Director's Playbook

About This Playbook
Quick Play Summary
Schema of Scenes
Auditions
The Play
Glossary
Producer Tasks
Pre-Production
Stage Management
Scheduling
Customized Scripts

edited by Sasha Newborn

BANDANNA BOOKS • 2014 • SANTA BARBARA

ISBN 978-0-942208-77-1

Shakespeare Directors Playbook Series

www.shakespeareplaybook.com

Hamlet **Merchant of Venice** **Twelfth Night** **Romeo and Juliet** **Taming of the Shrew** **A Midsummer Night's Dream** **Henry V** **As You Like It** **Richard III** **Much Ado About Nothing** **Othello** **Macbeth** **Antony and Cleopatra** **King Lear**

also

7 Plays with Transgenders **Falstaff: 4 Plays** **Venus and Adonis**

Sport, Adventure, Fantasy

The First Detective: 3 Stories. Poe **Hadji Murad,** Tolstoy **Frankenstein,** Mary Shelley **Surfing,** Jack London **Ski,** Doyle

History

Mitos y Leyendas/Myths and Legends of Mexico. Bilingual
The Beechers Through the 19th Century
Uncle Tom's Cabin, Harriet Beecher Stowe

Schooling

Don't Panic: Procrastinator's Guide to Writing a Term Paper
First Person Intense **Ghazals of Ghalib**
The Gospel According to Tolstoy **Gandhi on the *Gita***
The Everlasting Gospel, Blake **Italian for Opera Lovers**

Love

Dante & His Circle **Vita Nuova** **Sappho**
Aurora Leigh, Elizabeth Barrett Browning

Teachers Only

(*Q & A, glossaries, critical comments*)
Areopagitica **Apology of Socrates, & Crito** **Sappho**
Leaves of Grass, Whitman **Uncle Tom's Cabin,** H.B. Stowe

Contents

About This Playbook

This book is designed for prospective *directors, assistant directors—also producers*. More than half of the pages are waiting for you to fill in with your vision of the play, down to actors, details of sets, auditions, budget, schedule, program, etc.

Free downloads for large-type actors' scripts : *shakespeareplaybook.com/learscripts/*

Director's Tasks

If you've successfully directed plays before, you can skip this section.
Otherwise, here are some points to consider:

• A Director knows **how to delegate**. So many details... The first step might be to split responsibilities with a producer and assistant director.

• A Director is willing to make **hard choices**, such as assigning major roles.

• A Director **inspires confidence**. Being fair but businesslike is a start. Creating a team that can work together, so that all feel a sense of accomplishment—ideal. Demand hard work and reward people when it pays off.

• A Director's overall **vision of the play** helps others understand how they fit in. Shakespeare himself took wide latitude in choosing the setting to explore these themes. You can do the same—futuristic, modern, or period piece. Answer this question—Why are you doing this play now, for this audience? It may be simply for fun, to give a chance to aspiring actors to try out some roles. Or perhaps you want to reflect on recent current events with an appropriate production. In any case, share your conception to let the costumer, set designer, actors participate in, and perhaps improve on, that shared vision.

• A Director is a coach, an administrator, a front person, fundraiser, organizer, boss, den mother, and is invested in every person backstage or onstage.

• As for the book itself, a large swath of blank paper has been reserved for you throughout to keep your teeming brain in check. Make this *your* playbook. Fill it with sketches, notes, costume design, sets, scenery, props, expressions, actions—ideas good and bad, just as Orson Welles or Alfred Hitchcock did in preparing for a production. That's the fun part. Scenes have a blank stage diagram for sketching in sets. As for costume ideas, that's up to the director and the costume designer.

• Certain decisions must be considered before production can begin. Is there enough money or the prospect of getting the funds necessary—and on the other side, how much will it cost? Will all the actors be volunteers? The crew? The equipment, costumes, sets, props? How much time is required before opening night? You'll find those nuts and bolts pages to fill in, in the back section, along with some suggestions for creating a program, promotion, and such.

• Once the big decision—**to go ahead**—has been made, however, the "directorial" part of being a director comes into play.

• **The arc.** What's this play about? A battle for an empire or a love story? That's the reason for this playbook—as you start to fill in your conception of the play, act by act, you will also begin unconsciously characterizing the roles—who is in charge, will the match ultimately be a successful one?

• **Audition:** As you begin to *see* these characters in your mind, you can start filling in the Audition section. Although the title character carries the play, several strong roles also need filled by capable actors. The love story happens to be right in the middle of momentous historical events.

Act One: Kent and Gloucester discuss King Lear's plan to divide his kingdom in three parts for his daughters. As each speaks her love for him, Goneril and Regan use overblown language. Cordelia speaks honestly, which outrages Lear, who denies her inheritance. Kent tries to dissuade him, but Lear is stubborn; instead, he banishes Kent. One of Cordelia's suitors is willing to take her without any dowry. Regan and Goneril, observing Lear's erratic behavior, fear that he might take similar actions against themselves. Gloucester's older son Edmund (a bastard), plots to discredit his brother Edgar, the legitimate heir, with a false letter. Kent goes into disguise to continue serving Lear. Traveling to Goneril's, Lear is refused hospitality. The Fool joins Lear's party.

Act Two: Edmund urges Edgar to flee, which simply makes Gloucester suspect the worst; Edgar disguises himself as a naked madman. Edmund stabs his own arm to simulate Edgar's intentions. Kent and Oswald get in a tiff; Kent is put in stocks. Regan, like Goneril, refuses to host Lear and his company. A storm is brewing.

Act Three: Lear on the heath shouts his anger to the skies, showing signs of old age mental distress. Dialogues with the Fool, and later with the disguised Edgar, make Lear seem like the sane one. Lear now has flashes of sense, and regret for his decisions. Gloucester confides privately to Edmund his support of Lear; Edmund sees this letter as his opportunity to portray his father as a threat to the inheritors—and if his father loses, he, Edmund, will gain. Gloucester warns Lear of the threat on his life. Cornwall, Regan and Goneril are enraged, and when Gloucester comes home, he is bound and his eyes gouged out. One servant is killed, Cornwall is wounded.

Act Four: Gloucester also wanders on the heath, where Edgar finds him. Goneril returns home to find that Albany is not sympathetic to her side. Goneril begins to see Edmund as a suitable partner. Albany berates her. News comes that Cornwall has died, and Albany learns about Gloucester losing his eyes. The French have advanced with military forces; Cordelia is the Queen, and weeping over her sisters' actions. Lear is found, dressed oddly and delirious. Regan is suspicious on learning that Goneril is writing to Edmund. She, too, has eyes for Edmund. Edgar, still disguised, leads Gloucester to, he believes, the high cliffs of Dover, to commit suicide. Edgar, however, fools him into believing the level ground is a cliff; and that, once he jumped and fell on his face, that he had survived the steep fall—therefore he must live. Lear appears. When Cordelia's men reach him, he runs away. Oswald finds Gloucester to kill him, but Edgar fights and Oswald, dying, gives him a letter intended for Edmund from Goneril. In the French camp, Cordelia and a doctor revive Lear, who is unclear in his mind.

Act Five: In the British camp, Regan tests Edmund's feelings. Edgar speaks privately to Albany to set up a tourney. Edmund finds that he has professed love to both sisters, but is undecided. In a brief battle, the British side wins. Edgar leads Gloucester away to safety. Lear and Cordelia are led away as captives. Edmund gives secret instructions to a Captain to do them in. Albany, having read Goneril's letter, arrests Edmund for treason. A trumpet will call for combat; Edgar comes at the third trumpet to challenge Edmund, and defeats him. The dying Edmund confesses. Goneril's letter is shown. Edgar reveals himself. Goneril kills herself after having poisoned her sister Regan. Edmund asks that a messenger be sent to stop the murder of Cordelia. Too late. She is brought in dead, and Lear keeps imagining her alive. Edmund himself dies of his wound. Lear himself, with a last speech, also dies.

Entrances and Exits

Summary of actors entering and exiting in each scene.

Act One

1 *King Lear's Palace*

> Kent
> Gloucester
> Edmund

> Attendant
> Lear
> Duke of Albany
> Duke of Cornwall
> Goneril
> Regan
> Cordelia
> Followers
< Gloucester
< Edmund

> Gloucester
> France
> Burgundy
> Attendants

< Lear
< Burgundy
< Cornwall
< Albany
< Gloucester
< Attendants

< France
< Cordelia

< Goneril
< Regan

2 *The Earl of Gloucester's Castle*

> Edmund

> Gloucester
< Gloucester

> Edgar
< Edgar
< Edmund

3 *The Duke of Albany's Palace*

> Goneril
> Oswald
< Both

4 *The Duke of Albany's Palace*

> Kent
> Lear
> Attendants
< One Attendant
< Second Attendant

> Oswald <
< A Knight > <
< Third Attendant
> Oswald <
> Fool
> Goneril
> Albany
< Lear > <
< Kent
< Attendants
< Fool
> Oswald <
< All

5 *Court before the Duke of Albany's Palace*
> Lear
> Kent
> Fool
< Kent
> Gentleman
< All

Act Two

1 *A court within the Castle of the Earl of Gloucester*
> Edmund
> Curan <

> Edgar <

> Gloucester
> Servants
< some Servants

> Cornwall
> Regan
> Attendants
< All

2 *Before Gloucester's Castle*
> Kent
> Oswald

> Edmund
> Gloucester
> Cornwall
> Regan
> Servants
< Oswald
< Edmund
< Cornwall
< Regan
< Servants
< Gloucester
< Kent (asleep)

3 *The open country*
> Edgar <

4 *Before Gloucester's Castle*
> Kent (in stocks)
> Lear
> Fool
> Gentleman
< Lear

> Lear
> Gloucester <
> Cornwall
> Regan
> Gloucester
> Servants
> Oswald

> Goneril
< Lear
< Gloucester
< Kent
< Fool
> Gloucester
< All

Act Three

1 *A heath. Storm continues*
> Kent
> Gentleman
< Both

2 *Another part of the heath*
> Lear
> Fool
> Kent <
< Lear
< Fool

3 *Gloucester's Castle*
> Gloucester
> Edmund
< Gloucester
< Edmund

4 *The heath. Before a hovel*
> Lear
> Kent
> Fool < >
> Edgar
> Gloucester
< All

5 *Gloucester's Castle*
> Cornwall
> Edmund
< Both

6 *A farmhouse near Gloucester's Castle*
> Gloucester
> Lear
> Kent
> Fool
> Edgar
< Gloucester
> Gloucester <
< Lear
< Kent
< Fool

< Edgar

7 *Gloucester's Castle*
> Cornwall
> Regan
> Goneril
> Edmund
> Servants
< some Servants
> Oswald
< Goneril
< Edmund
< Oswald
< other Servants
< First Servant (dies)
<Servant
< Gloucester
< Cornwall
< Regan
< All

Act Four
1 *The heath*
> Edgar
> Gloucester
> Old Man <
< Both

2 *Before the Duke of Albany's Palace*

> Goneril
> Edmund
> Oswald
< Edmund
< Oswald

> Albany
> Gentleman
< Goneril
< All

3 *The French camp near Dover*

> Kent
> Gentleman
< Both

4 *The French camp*

> Cordelia
> Doctor
> Soldiers
< an Officer
> Messenger
< All

5 *Gloucester's Castle*

> Regan
> Oswald
< Both

6 *The country near Dover*

> Gloucester
> Edgar

>Lear

> Gentleman
> Attendants

< Lear (running)
< Attendants

< Gentleman

> Oswald
< Oswald (dies)

< All

7 *A tent in the French camp*

> Cordelia
> Kent
> Doctor
> Gentleman

> Lear (carried)
< Cordelia
< Doctor
< Lear

< Gentleman
< Kent

Act Five

1 *The British camp near Dover*

> Edmund
> Regan
> Gentleman
> Soldiers
< an Officer

> Albany
> Goneril
> Soldiers

> Edgar
< Goneril
< Edmund
< Regan
< Gentleman
< Soldiers

< Edgar
> Edmund
< Albany
< Edmund

2 *A field between the two camps*

> Edgar
> Gloucester
< Edgar >
< Both

3 *The British camp, near Dover*

> Edmund
> Lear
> Cordelia
> Soldiers
> Captain
< Lear
< Cordelia

< Captain
> Albany
> Goneril
> Regan
> Soldiers

< Regan
> Herald
> Edgar

< Goneril
< Officer

> Gentleman

> Kent
< Gentleman

> Goneril (dead)
> Regan (dead)

< Edgar
< Edmund (carried)
> Lear
> Cordelia (dead)
> Edgar
> Captain
> Soldiers
> Second Captain
< Lear (dies)
< All

Auditions

Advice specific to this play: The actual timeframe of this story is not specific, which leaves a lot of room for imaginative sets or costumes. The story involves extreme family relationships-from-hell. Even Cordelia is somewhat snippy. Backstabbing, conniving, disguise, displaced aggression—is it a madhouse, or just ordinary life writ large?

Some directors use "cold" readings (unrehearsed) for first auditions. Then, if the actor is worth a second call, assign a few pages to rehearse, so that you can hear a more nuanced reading perhaps paired up to test personal chemistry of actors in dialogue.

Auditions for the **major roles should be done early** in the process. As you become familiar with these actors, you can better visualize scenes, and thus begin to flesh out the vision of the drama, with your available talent. Equally important, the actors begin to bond among themselves as part of *the cast.*

Prepare **understudies** for the major roles, so that, if the occasion arises, they are prepared to step in at the last minute. Do *you* have an understudy, an assistant director? Doing Shakespeare is a learning experience for everyone.

Should everyone see everything? No need, but *someone* must be in charge of scheduling and reminders.

This play has a number of opportunities for extras. Though they have few or no lines, they at least need to know when and where to position themselves.

As director, you have the **prerogative to make changes** in the play as you see fit—from costuming and set design to cutting lines that don't work, sometimes (gasp) cutting whole scenes or characters—anything that makes the play work better.

Acting Tips

Memorizing lines. Shakespeare loves language, and he often gives lengthy speeches even for minor characters. How to cope? Here are three tips from the pros: 1) write it out in longhand, which forces your mind and hand to give attention to every word. 2) record the speech, play back and repeat the lines. 3) rehearse standing up, speaking in character with gestures, so that your whole body participates.

Voice. Use your diaphragm for better breath control, and power when you need it. Can you project even with a stage whisper to the audience?

On stage. Hit your marks; know where to stand, when to move. Face the audience when speaking. Stay in character; don't wait until your speech to react to others. Jitters? Use that energy to animate your participation.

If you forget a line during a performance, don't stop. Stay in character and use your own words for what the character would say in that scene, until you get back on track.

Pay attention to the Director's vision of the whole. How does the director intend to "frame" the play—modern? classical? parody of current politician scandals? Goofy slapstick? Inevitable, or cliff-hanging in every scene? Your role ought to fit right in with all the others. Shakespeare offers great variety and even subtlety for actors.

CANDIDATES FOR ROLES

Fill in your choices:

Lear

Lear understudy

Edmund

Edgar

Gloucester

Goneril

Regan

Cordelia

Cornwall

Albany

Burgundy

France

Kent

Fool

Oswald

Knight

Gentleman

Curan

Old Man

Doctor

Herald

Captains

Extras and Groups

Officers

Soldiers

Messenger

Attendants

Crew

Who is on your Crew? Each of these functions may require a budget for expenses, or need for volunteers or helpers. Find out ahead of time. And what happens to sets, costumes, tools, etc. after the play is over? Who owns what, and who is responsible for disposal? Set a policy appropriate for your venue.

Assistant director: advisor to director, taking care of details, able to step in if necessary.

Producer: in charge of the business end: budget, ticket office, ushers, money, fundraising (if necessary), publicity, program, theater rental.

Costume Designer: wardrobe for the cast

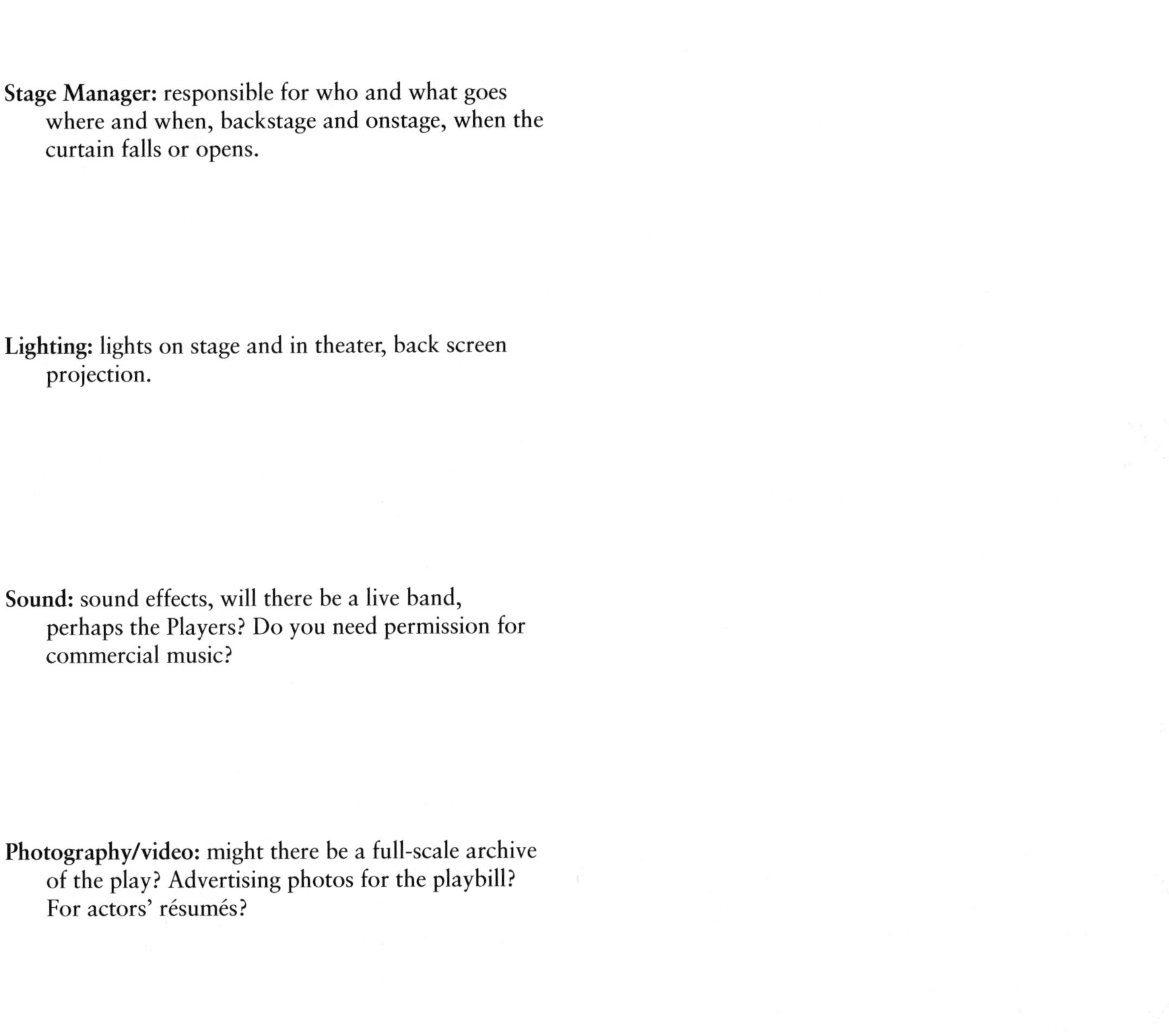

Set Designer: moveable sets, backdrops, materials, props

Stage Manager: responsible for who and what goes where and when, backstage and onstage, when the curtain falls or opens.

Lighting: lights on stage and in theater, back screen projection.

Sound: sound effects, will there be a live band, perhaps the Players? Do you need permission for commercial music?

Photography/video: might there be a full-scale archive of the play? Advertising photos for the playbill? For actors' résumés?

Act One

1

[King Lear's Palace]

[Enter Kent, Gloucester, and Edmund]

[Kent and Gloucester converse. Edmund stands back]

Kent. I thought the King had more affected the Duke of Albany than Cornwall.

Gloucester. It did always seem so to us; but now, in the division of the kingdom, it appears not which of the Dukes he values most, for equalities are so weighed that curiosity in neither can make choice of either's moiety.

Kent. Is not this your son, my lord?

Gloucester. His breeding, sir, has been at my charge. I have so often blushed to acknowledge him that now I am brazed to it.

Kent. I cannot conceive you.

Gloucester. Sir, this young fellow's mother could; whereupon she grew round-wombed, and had indeed, sir, a son for her cradle before she had a husband for her bed. Do you smell a fault?

Kent. I cannot wish the fault undone, the issue of it being so proper.

Gloucester. But I have, sir, a son by order of law, some year elder than this, who yet is no dearer in my account. Though this knave came something saucily into the world before he was sent for, yet was his mother fair, there was good sport at his making, and the whoreson must be acknowledged.
Do you know this noble gentleman, Edmund?

Edmund. [*comes forward*] No, my lord.

Gloucester. My Lord of Kent. Remember him hereafter as my honorable friend.

Edmund. My services to your lordship.

Kent. I must love you, and sue to know you better.

Edmund. Sir, I shall study deserving.

Gloucester. He has been out nine years, and away he shall again.

[Sound a sennet]

The King is coming.

I have so often blushed to acknowledge him that now I am brazed to it

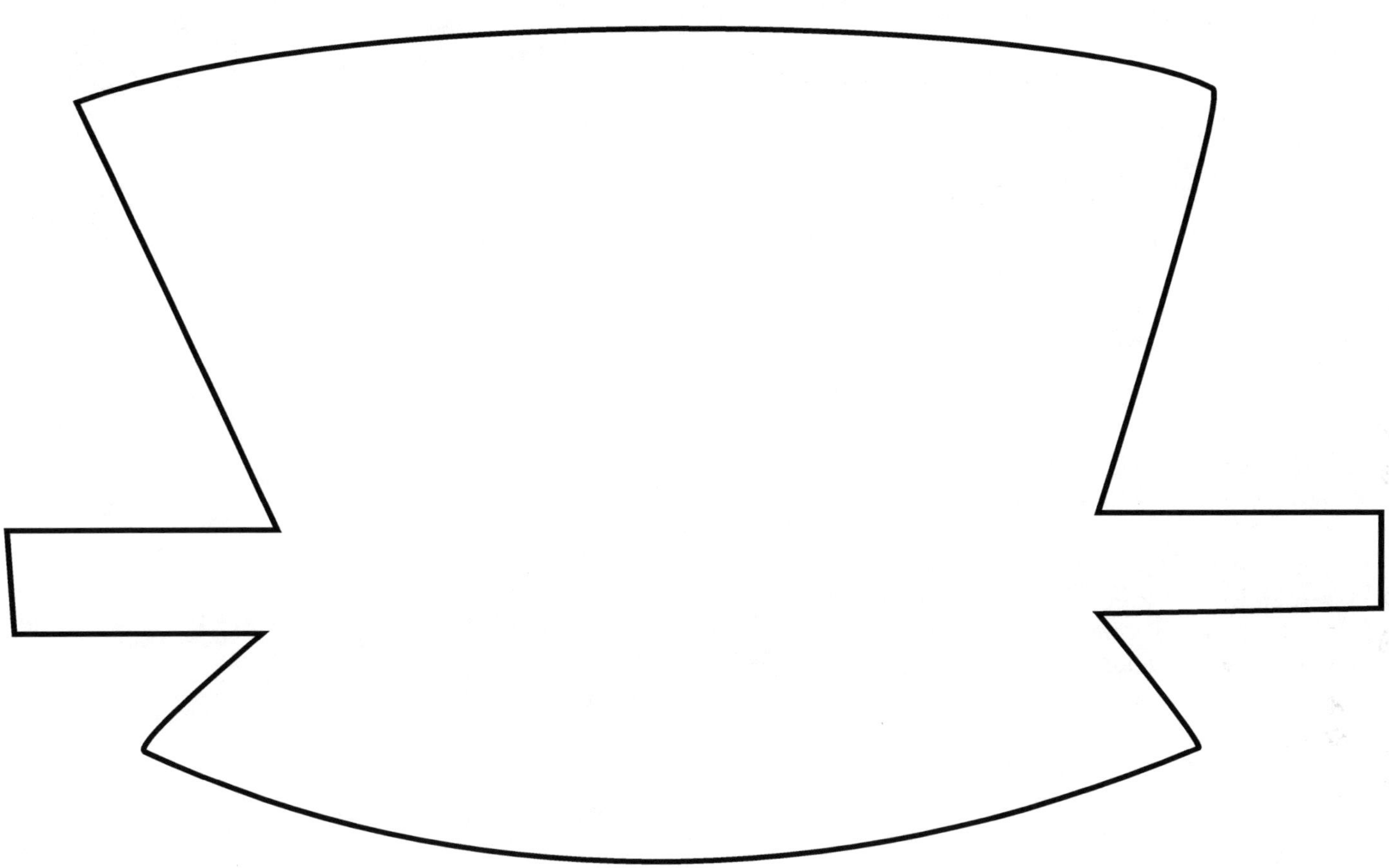

[Enter one bearing a coronet; then Lear; then the Dukes of Albany and Cornwall; next, Goneril, Regan, Cordelia, with Followers.

Lear. Attend the lords of France and Burgundy, Gloucester.

Gloucester. I shall, my liege.

[Exeunt Gloucester and Edmund]

Lear. Meantime we shall express our darker purpose.
Give me the map there. Know we have divided
In three our kingdom; and it is our fast intent
To shake all cares and business from our age,
Conferring them on younger strengths while we
Unburdened crawl toward death. Our son of Cornwall,
And you, our no less loving son of Albany,
We have this hour a constant will to publish
Our daughters' several dowers, that future strife
May be prevented now. The princes, France and Burgundy,
Great rivals in our youngest daughter's love,
Long in our court have made their amorous sojourn,
And here are to be answered. Tell me, my daughters
(Since now we will divest us both of rule,
Interest of territory, cares of state),
Which of you shall we say does love us most?
That we our largest bounty may extend
Where nature does with merit challenge. Goneril,
Our eldest-born, speak first.

Goneril. Sir, I love you more than words can wield the matter;
Dearer than eyesight, space, and liberty;
Beyond what can be valued, rich or rare;
No less than life, with grace, health, beauty, honor;
As much as child ever loved, or father found;
A love that makes breath poor, and speech unable.
Beyond all manner of so much I love you.

Cordelia. [*Aside*] What shall Cordelia speak? Love, and be silent.

Lear. Of all these bounds, even from this line to this,
With shadowy forests and with champains riched,
With plenteous rivers and wide-skirted meads,
We make you lady. To yours and Albany's issue
Be this perpetual.
What says our second daughter,
Our dearest Regan, wife to Cornwall? Speak.

Regan. Sir, I am made
Of the selfsame metal that my sister is,
And prize me at her worth. In my true heart
I find she names my very deed of love;
Only she comes too short, that I profess

Know we have divided
In three our kingdom

Myself an enemy to all other joys
Which the most precious square of sense possesses,
And find I am alone felicitate
In your dear Highness' love.

Cordelia. [*Aside*] Then poor Cordelia!
And yet not so; since I am sure my love's
More richer than my tongue.

Lear. To you and yours hereditary ever
Remain this ample third of our fair kingdom,
No less in space, validity, and pleasure
Than that conferred on Goneril.—

Lear. Now, our joy,
Although the last, not least; to whose young love
The vines of France and milk of Burgundy
Strive to be interest; what can you say to draw
A third more opulent than your sisters? Speak.

Cordelia. Nothing, my lord.

Lear. Nothing?

Cordelia. Nothing.

Lear. Nothing can come of nothing. Speak again.

Cordelia. Unhappy that I am, I cannot heave
My heart into my mouth. I love your Majesty
According to my bond; no more nor less.

Lear. How, how, Cordelia? Mend your speech a little,
Lest it may mar your fortunes.

Cordelia. Good my lord,
You have begot me, bred me, loved me; I
Return those duties back as are right fit,
Obey you, love you, and most honor you.
Why have my sisters husbands, if they say
They love you all? Haply, when I shall wed,
That lord whose hand must take my plight shall carry
Half my love with him, half my care and duty.
Sure I shall never marry like my sisters,
To love my father all.

Lear. But goes your heart with this?

Cordelia. Ay, good my lord.

Lear. So young, and so untender?

Cordelia. So young, my lord, and true.

Lear. Let it be so! Your truth then be your dower!
For, by the sacred radiance of the sun,
The mysteries of Hecate and the night;
By all the operation of the orbs
From whom we do exist and cease to be;
Here I disclaim all my paternal care,
Propinquity and property of blood,
And as a stranger to my heart and me
Hold you from this forever. The barbarous Scythian,
Or he that makes his generation messes
To gorge his appetite, shall to my bosom
Be as well neighbored, pitied, and relieved,
As you my sometime daughter.

Kent. Good my liege—

How, how, Cordelia? Mend your speech a little,
Lest it may mar your fortunes.

Lear. Peace, Kent!
Come not between the dragon and his wrath.
I loved her most, and thought to set my rest
On her kind nursery.— Hence and avoid my sight!—
So be my grave my peace as here I give
Her father's heart from her! Call France! Who stirs?
Call Burgundy! Cornwall and Albany,
With my two daughters' dowers digest this third;
Let pride, which she calls plainness, marry her.
I do invest you jointly in my power,
Preeminence, and all the large effects
That troop with majesty. Ourself, by monthly course,
With reservation of an hundred knights,
By you to be sustained, shall our abode
Make with you by due turns. Only we still retain
The name, and all the additions to a king. The sway,
Revenue, execution of the rest,
Beloved sons, be yours; which to confirm,
This coronet part between you.

Kent. Royal Lear,
Whom I have ever honored as my king,
Loved as my father, as my master followed,
As my great patron thought on in my prayers—

Lear. The bow is bent and drawn; make from the shaft.

Kent. Let it fall rather, though the fork invade
The region of my heart! Be Kent unmannerly
When Lear is mad. What would you do, old man?
Think you that duty shall have dread to speak
When power to flattery bows? To plainness honor's bound
When majesty falls to folly. Reverse your doom;
And in your best consideration check
This hideous rashness. Answer my life my judgment,
Your youngest daughter does not love you least,
Nor are those empty-hearted whose low sound
Reverbs no hollowness.

Lear. Kent, on your life, no more!

Kent. My life I never held but as a pawn
To wage against your enemies; nor fear to lose it,
Your safety being the motive.

Lear. Out of my sight!

To plainness honor's bound
When majesty falls to folly

Kent. See better, Lear, and let me still remain
The true blank of your eye.

Lear. Now by Apollo—

Kent. Now by Apollo, King,
You swear your gods in vain.

Lear. O vassal! miscreant!

[*Lays his hand on his sword*]

Albany, Cornwall. Dear sir, forbear!

Kent. Do!
Kill your physician, and the fee bestow
Upon the foul disease. Revoke your gift,
Or, while I can vent clamour from my throat,
I'll tell you you do evil.

Lear. Hear me, recreant!
On your allegiance, hear me!
Since you have sought to make us break our vow—
Which we dare never yet— and with strained pride
To come between our sentence and our power,—
Which nor our nature nor our place can bear,—
Our potency made good, take your reward.
Five days we do allot you for provision
To shield you from diseases of the world,
And on the sixth to turn your hated back
Upon our kingdom. If, on the tenth day following,
Your banished trunk be found in our dominions,
The moment is your death. Away! By Jupiter,
This shall not be revoked.

Kent. Fare you well, King. Since thus you will appear,
Freedom lives hence, and banishment is here.
[*To Cordelia*] The gods to their dear shelter take you, maid,
That justly think and have most rightly said!
[*To Regan and Goneril*] And your large speeches may your deeds approve,
That good effects may spring from words of love.
Thus Kent, O princes, bids you all adieu;
He'll shape his old course in a country new.

[*Exit Kent*]

If, on the tenth day following,
Your banished trunk be found in our dominions,
The moment is your death.

[*Flourish. Enter Gloucester, with France and Burgundy; Attendants*]

Gloucester. Here's France and Burgundy, my noble lord.

Lear. My Lord of Burgundy,
We first address toward you, who with this king
Have rivalled for our daughter. What in the least
Will you require in present dower with her,
Or cease your quest of love?

Burgundy. Most royal Majesty,
I crave no more than has your Highness offered,
Nor will you tender less.

Lear. Right noble Burgundy,
When she was dear to us, we did hold her so;
But now her price is fallen. Sir, there she stands.
If aught within that little seeming substance,
Or all of it, with our displeasure pieced,
And nothing more, may fitly like your Grace,
She's there, and she is yours.

Burgundy. I know no answer.

Lear. Will you, with those infirmities she owes,
Unfriended, new adopted to our hate,
Dowered with our curse, and strangered with our oath,
Take her, or leave her?

Burgundy. Pardon me, royal sir.
Election makes not up on such conditions.

Lear. Then leave her, sir; for, by the power that made me,
I tell you all her wealth. [*To France*] For you, great King,
I would not from your love make such a stray
To match you where I hate; therefore beseech you
To avert your liking a more worthier way
Than on a wretch whom nature is ashamed
Almost to acknowledge hers.

When she was dear to us, we did hold her so;
But now her price is fallen.

France. This is most strange,
That she that even but now was your best object,
The argument of your praise, balm of your age,
Most best, most dearest, should in this trice of time
Commit a thing so monstrous to dismantle
So many folds of favor. Sure her offence
Must be of such unnatural degree
That monsters it, or your fore-vouched affection
Fallen into taint; which to believe of her
Must be a faith that reason without miracle
Should never plant in me.

Cordelia. I yet beseech your Majesty,
If for I want that glib and oily art
To speak and purpose not, since what I well intend,
I'll do it before I speak— that you make known
It is no vicious blot, murder, or foulness,
No unchaste action or dishonored step,
That has deprived me of your grace and favor;
But even for want of that for which I am richer—
A still-soliciting eye, and such a tongue
As I am glad I have not, though not to have it
Have lost me in your liking.

Lear. Better you had not been born than not to have pleased me better.

France. Is it but this— a tardiness in nature
Which often leaves the history unspoke
That it intends to do? My Lord of Burgundy,
What say you to the lady? Love's not love
When it is mingled with regards that stands
Aloof from the entire point. Will you have her?
She is herself a dowry.

Burgundy. Royal Lear,
Give but that portion which yourself proposed,
And here I take Cordelia by the hand,
Duchess of Burgundy.

Lear. Nothing! I have sworn; I am firm.

Burgundy. I am sorry then you have so lost a father
That you must lose a husband.

Cordelia. Peace be with Burgundy!
Since that respects of fortune are his love,
I shall not be his wife.

such a tongue
As I am glad I have not, though not to have it
Have lost me in your liking.

France. Fairest Cordelia, that are most rich, being poor;
Most choice, forsaken; and most loved, despised!
You and your virtues here I seize upon.
Be it lawful I take up what's cast away.
Gods, gods! it is strange that from their coldest neglect
My love should kindle to inflamed respect.
Your dowerless daughter, King, thrown to my chance,
Is queen of us, of ours, and our fair France.
Not all the dukes in waterish Burgundy
Can buy this unprized precious maid of me.
Bid them farewell, Cordelia, though unkind.
You lose here, a better where to find.

Lear. You have her, France; let her be yours; for we
Have no such daughter, nor shall ever see
That face of hers again. Therefore be gone
Without our grace, our love, our benison.
Come, noble Burgundy.

[*Flourish*]

[*Exeunt Lear, Burgundy, Cornwall, Albany,
Gloucester, and Attendants*]

France. Bid farewell to your sisters.

Cordelia. The jewels of our father, with washed eyes
Cordelia leaves you. I know you what you are;
And, like a sister, am most loath to call
Your faults as they are named. Use well our father.
To your professed bosoms I commit him;
But yet, alas, stood I within his grace,
I would prefer him to a better place!
So farewell to you both.

Goneril. Prescribe not us our duties.

Regan. Let your study
Be to content your lord, who has received you
At fortune's alms. You have obedience scanted,
And well are worth the want that you have wanted.

Cordelia. Time shall unfold what plighted cunning hides.
Who cover faults, at last shame them derides.
Well may you prosper!

France. Come, my fair Cordelia.

[*Exeunt France and Cordelia*]

You have her, France; let her be yours; for we
Have no such daughter, nor shall ever see
That face of hers again.

Goneril. Sister, it is not little I have to say of what most nearly appertains to us both. I think our father will hence tonight.

Regan. That's most certain, and with you; next month with us.

Goneril. You see how full of changes his age is. The observation we have made of it has not been little. He always loved our sister most, and with what poor judgment he has now cast her off appears too grossly.

Regan. It's the infirmity of his age; yet he has ever but slenderly known himself.

Goneril. The best and soundest of his time has been but rash; then must we look to receive from his age, not alone the imperfections of long-ingraffed condition, but therewithal the unruly waywardness that infirm and choleric years bring with them.

Regan. Such unconstant starts are we like to have from him as this of Kent's banishment.

Goneril. There is further compliment of leave-taking between France and him. Pray you let's hit together. If our father carry authority with such dispositions as he bears, this last surrender of his will but offend us.

Regan. We shall further think on it.

Goneril. We must do something, and in the heat.

[*Exeunt*]

Pray you let's hit together. If our father carry authority with such dispositions as he bears, this last surrender of his will but offend us.

2

[*The Earl of Gloucester's Castle*]

[*Enter Edmund the Bastard alone, with a letter*]

Edmund. You, Nature, are my goddess; to your law
My services are bound. Wherefore should I
Stand in the plague of custom, and permit
The curiosity of nations to deprive me,
For that I am some twelve or fourteen moonshines
Lag of a brother? Why bastard? wherefore base?
When my dimensions are as well compact,
My mind as generous, and my shape as true,
As honest madam's issue? Why brand they us
With base? with baseness? bastardy? base, base?
Who, in the lusty stealth of nature, take
More composition and fierce quality
Than does, within a dull, stale, tired bed,
Go to the creating a whole tribe of fops
Got between asleep and wake? Well then,
Legitimate Edgar, I must have your land.
Our father's love is to the bastard Edmund
As to the legitimate. Fine word— "legitimate"!
Well, my legitimate, if this letter speed,
And my invention thrive, Edmund the base
Shall top the legitimate. I grow; I prosper.
Now, gods, stand up for bastards!

[*Enter Gloucester*]

Gloucester. Kent banished thus? and France in choler parted?
And the King gone tonight? subscribed his power?
Confined to exhibition? All this done
Upon the gad? Edmund, how now? What news?

Why bastard? wherefore base?
When my dimensions are as well compact,
My mind as generous, and my shape as true

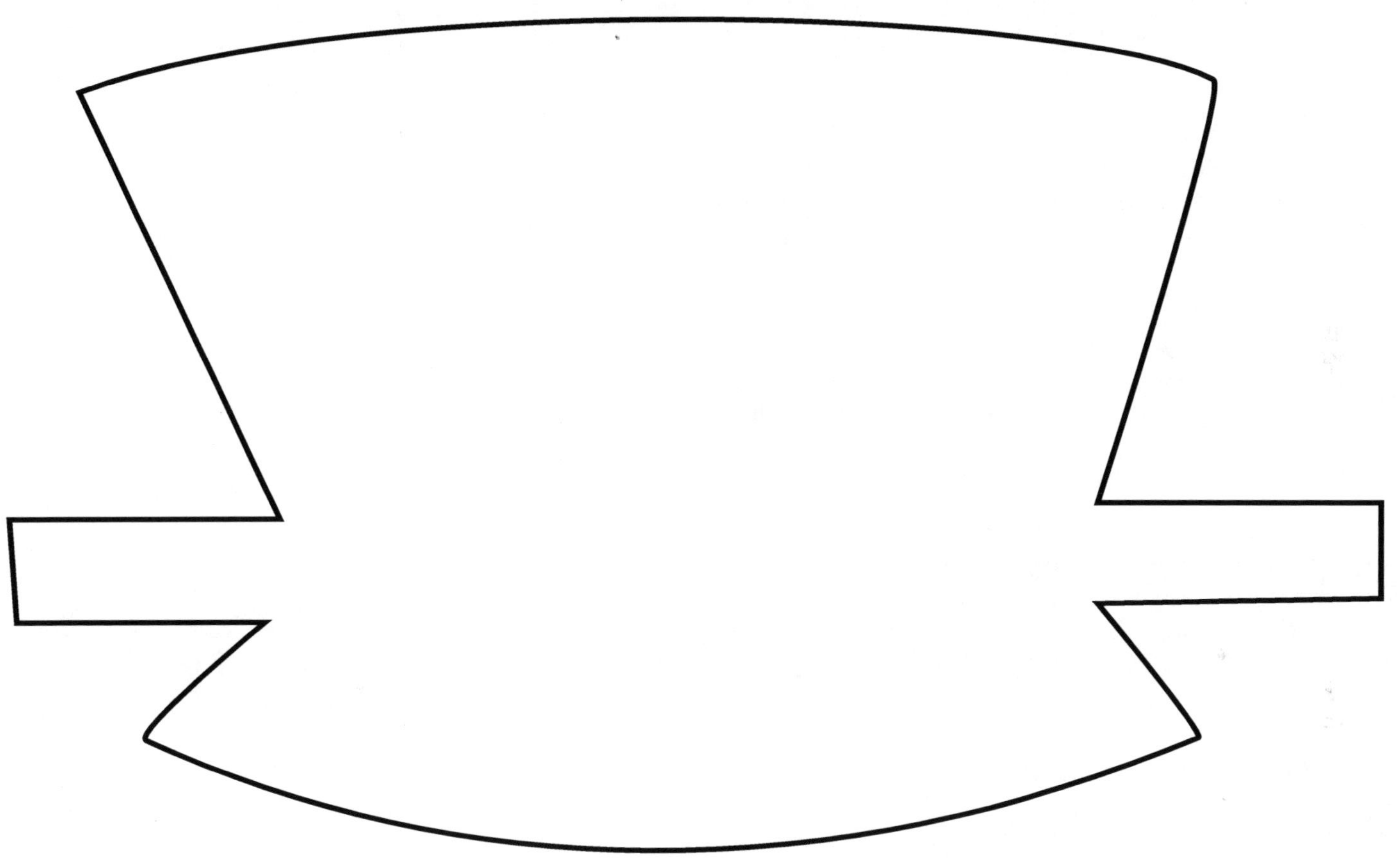

Edmund. So please your lordship, none.

[*Puts up the letter*]

Gloucester. Why so earnestly seek you to put up that letter?

Edmund. I know no news, my lord.

Gloucester. What paper were you reading?

Edmund. Nothing, my lord.

Gloucester. No? What needed then that terrible dispatch of it into your pocket? The quality of nothing has not such need to hide itself. Let's see. Come, if it be nothing, I shall not need spectacles.

Edmund. I beseech you, sir, pardon me. It is a letter from my brother that I have not all over-read; and for so much as I have perused, I find it not fit for your overlooking.

Gloucester. Give me the letter, sir.

Edmund. I shall offend, either to detain or give it. The contents, as in part I understand them, are to blame.

Gloucester. Let's see, let's see!

Edmund. I hope, for my brother's justification, he wrote this but as an essay or test of my virtue.

Gloucester. (reads)

"This policy and reverence of age makes the world bitter to the best of our times; keeps our fortunes from us till our oldness cannot relish them. I begin to find an idle and fond bondage in the oppression of aged tyranny, who sways, not as it has power, but as it is suffered. Come to me, that of this I may speak more. If our father would sleep till I waked him, you should enjoy half his revenue forever, and live the beloved of your brother,

"Edgar."

Hum! Conspiracy? "Sleep till I waked him, you should enjoy half his revenue.' My son Edgar! Had he a hand to write this? a heart and brain to breed it in? When came this to you? Who brought it?

What needed then that terrible dispatch of it into your pocket? The quality of nothing has not such need to hide itself. Let's see.

Edmund. It was not brought me, my lord: there's the cunning of it. I found it thrown in at the casement of my closet.

Gloucester. You know the character to be your brother's?

Edmund. If the matter were good, my lord, I dare swear it were his; but in respect of that, I would fain think it were not.

Gloucester. It is his.

Edmund. It is his hand, my lord; but I hope his heart is not in the contents.

Gloucester. Has he never before sounded you in this business?

Edmund. Never, my lord. But I have heard him oft maintain it to be fit that, sons at perfect age, and fathers declining, the father should be as ward to the son, and the son manage his revenue.

Gloucester. O villain, villain! His very opinion in the letter! Abhorred villain! Unnatural, detested, brutish villain! worse than brutish! Go, sirrah, seek him. I'll apprehend him. Abominable villain! Where is he?

Edmund. I do not well know, my lord. If it shall please you to suspend your indignation against my brother till you can derive from him better testimony of his intent, you should run a certain course; where, if you violently proceed against him, mistaking his purpose, it would make a great gap in your own honor and shake in pieces the heart of his obedience. I dare pawn down my life for him that he has writ this to feel my affection to your honor, and to no other pretence of danger.

Gloucester. Think you so?

Edmund. If your honor judge it meet, I will place you where you shall hear us confer of this and by an auricular assurance have your satisfaction, and that without any further delay than this very evening.

I have heard him oft maintain it to be fit that, sons at perfect age, and fathers declining, the father should be as ward to the son

Gloucester. He cannot be such a monster.

Edmund. Nor is not, sure.

Gloucester. To his father, that so tenderly and entirely loves him. Heaven and earth! Edmund, seek him out; wind me into him, I pray you; frame the business after your own wisdom. I would unstate myself to be in a due resolution.

Edmund. I will seek him, sir, presently; convey the business as I shall find means, and acquaint you withal.

Gloucester. These late eclipses in the sun and moon portend no good to us. Though the wisdom of nature can reason it thus and thus, yet nature finds itself scourged by the sequent effects. Love cools, friendship falls off, brothers divide. In cities, mutinies; in countries, discord; in palaces, treason; and the bond cracked between son and father. This villain of mine comes under the prediction; there's son against father: the King falls from bias of nature; there's father against child. We have seen the best of our time. Machinations, hollowness, treachery, and all ruinous disorders follow us disquietly to our graves. Find out this villain, Edmund; it shall lose you nothing; do it carefully. And the noble and true-hearted Kent banished! His offence, honesty! It's strange.

[*Exit*]

Edmund. This is the excellent foppery of the world, that, when we are sick in fortune, often the surfeit of our own behavior, we make guilty of our disasters the sun, the moon, and the stars; as if we were villains on necessity; fools by heavenly compulsion; knaves, thieves, and treachers by spherical pre-dominance; drunkards, liars, and adulterers by an enforced obedience of planetary influence; and all that we are evil in, by a divine thrusting on. An admirable evasion of whore-master man, to lay his goatish disposition to the charge of a star! My father compounded with my mother under the Dragon's Tail, and my nativity was under Ursa Major, so that it follows I am rough and lecherous. Fut! I should have been that I am, had the maidenliest star in the firmament twinkled on my bastardizing. Edgar—

Machinations, hollowness, treachery, and all ruinous disorders follow us disquietly to our graves.

[*Enter Edgar*]

and pat! he comes, like the catastrophe of the old comedy. My cue is villainous melancholy, with a sigh like Tom of Bedlam. O, these eclipses do portend these divisions! Fa, sol, la, mi.

Edgar. How now, brother Edmund? What serious contemplation are you in?

Edmund. I am thinking, brother, of a prediction I read this other day, what should follow these eclipses.

Edgar. Do you busy yourself with that?

Edmund. I promise you, the effects he writes of succeed unhappily: as of unnaturalness between the child and the parent; death, dearth, dissolutions of ancient amities; divisions in state, menaces and maledictions against king and nobles; needless diffidences, banishment of friends, dissipation of cohorts, nuptial breaches, and I know not what.

Edgar. How long have you been a sectary astronomical?

Edmund. Come, come! When saw you my father last?

Edgar. The night gone by.

Edmund. Spoke you with him?

Edgar. Ay, two hours together.

Edmund. Parted you in good terms? Found you no displeasure in him by word or countenance?

Edgar. None at all.

Edmund. Bethink yourself wherein you may have offended him; and at my entreaty forbear his presence until some little time has qualified the heat of his displeasure, which at this instant so rages in him that with the mischief of your person it would scarcely allay.

Edgar. Some villain has done me wrong.

Edmund. That's my fear. I pray you have a continent forbearance till the speed of his rage goes slower; and, as I say, retire with me to my lodging, from whence I will fitly bring you to hear my lord speak. Pray you, go! There's my key. If you do stir abroad, go armed.

Edgar. Armed, brother?

Edmund. Brother, I advise you to the best. Go armed. I am no honest man if there be any good meaning toward you. I have told you what I have seen and heard; but faintly, nothing like the image and horror of it. Pray you, away!

Edgar. Shall I hear from you anon?

Edmund. I do serve you in this business.

[*Exit Edgar*]

Bethink yourself wherein you may have offended him; and at my entreaty forbear his presence

A credulous father! and a brother noble,
Whose nature is so far from doing harms
That he suspects none; on whose foolish honesty
My practices ride easy! I see the business.
Let me, if not by birth, have lands by wit;
All with me's meet that I can fashion fit.

[*Exit Edmund*]

3

[The Duke of Albany's Palace]

[Enter Goneril and her Steward Oswald]

Goneril. Did my father strike my gentleman for chiding
of his fool?

Oswald. Ay, madam.

Goneril. By day and night, he wrongs me! Every hour
He flashes into one gross crime or other
That sets us all at odds. I'll not endure it.
His knights grow riotous, and himself upbraids us
On every trifle. When he returns from hunting,
I will not speak with him. Say I am sick.
If you come slack of former services,
You shall do well; the fault of it I'll answer.

[Horns within]

Oswald. He's coming, madam; I hear him.

Goneril. Put on what weary negligence you please,
You and your fellows. I'd have it come to question.
If he distaste it, let him to our sister,
Whose mind and mine I know in that are one,
Not to be overruled. Idle old man,
That still would manage those authorities
That he has given away! Now, by my life,
Old fools are babes again, and must be used
With checks as flatteries, when they are seen abused.
Remember what I have said.

Oswald. Very well, madam.

Goneril. And let his knights have colder looks among
you.
What grows of it, no matter. Advise your fellows so.
I would breed from hence occasions, and I shall,
That I may speak. I'll write straight to my sister
To hold my very course. Prepare for dinner.

[Exeunt]

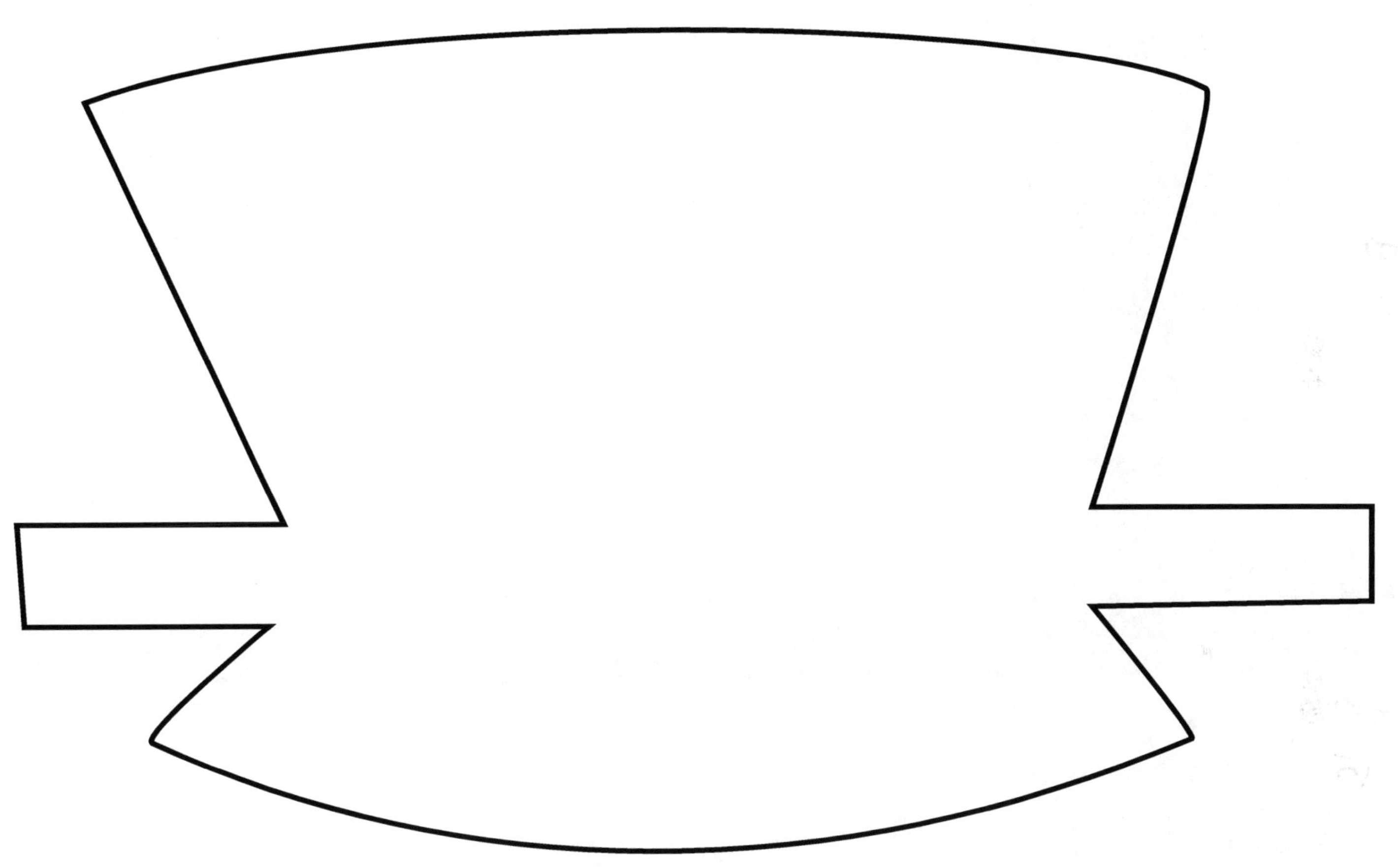

4

[The Duke of Albany's Palace]

[Enter Kent, disguised]

Kent. If but as well I other accents borrow,
That can my speech defuse, my good intent
May carry through itself to that full issue
For which I razed my likeness. Now, banished Kent,
If you can serve where you do stand condemned,
So may it come, your master, whom you love,
Shall find you full of labors.

[Horns within. Enter Lear, Knights, and Attendants]

Lear. Let me not stay a jot for dinner; go get it ready.

[Exit an Attendant]

How now? What are you?

Kent. A man, sir.

Lear. What do you profess? What would you with us?

Kent. I do profess to be no less than I seem, to serve him truly that will put me in trust, to love him that is honest, to converse with him that is wise and says little, to fear judgment, to fight when I cannot choose, and to eat no fish.

Lear. What are you?

Kent. A very honest-hearted fellow, and as poor as the King.

Lear. If you be as poor for a subject as he's for a king, you are poor enough. What would you?

Kent. Service.

Lear. Who would you serve?

Kent. You.

Lear. Do you know me, fellow?

Kent. No, sir; but you have that in your countenance which I would fain call master.

Lear. What's that?

Kent. Authority.

Lear. What services can you do?

Kent. I can keep honest counsel, ride, run, mar a curious tale in telling it and deliver a plain message bluntly. That which ordinary men are fit for, I am qualified in, and the best of me is diligence.

Lear. How old are you?

I do profess to be no less than I seem, to serve him truly that will put me in trust

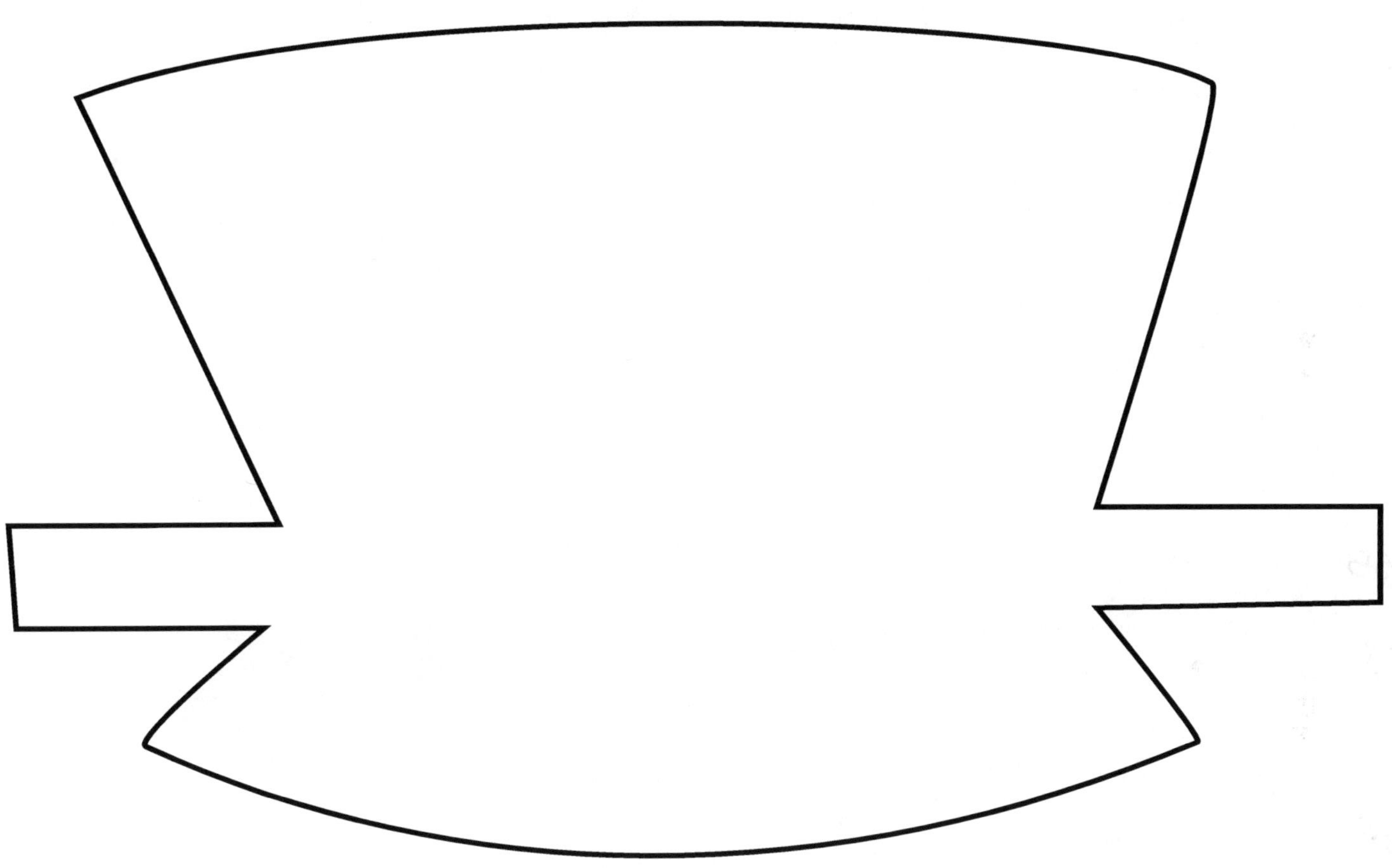

Kent. Not so young, sir, to love a woman for singing, nor so old to dote on her for anything. I have years on my back forty-eight.

Lear. Follow me; you shall serve me. If I like you no worse after dinner, I will not part from you yet. Dinner, ho, dinner! Where's my knave? my fool? Go you and call my fool here.

[*Exit an Attendant*]

[*Enter Oswald the Steward*]

You, you, sirrah, where's my daughter?

Oswald. So please you—

[*Exit Oswald*]

Lear. What says the fellow there? Call the clotpoll back.

[*Exit a Knight*]

Where's my fool, ho? I think the world's asleep.

[*Enter Knight*]

How now? Where's that mongrel?

Knight. He says, my lord, your daughter is not well.

Lear. Why came not the slave back to me when I called him?

Knight. Sir, he answered me in the roundest manner, he would not.

Lear. He would not?

Knight. My lord, I know not what the matter is; but to my judgment your Highness is not entertained with that ceremonious affection as you were wont. There's a great abatement of kindness appears as well in the general dependants as in the Duke himself also and your daughter.

Lear. Ha! say you so?

Knight. I beseech you pardon me, my lord, if I be mistaken; for my duty cannot be silent when I think your Highness wronged.

Lear. You but remember me of my own conception. I have perceived a most faint neglect of late, which I have rather blamed as my own jealous curiosity than as a very pretence and purpose of unkindness. I will look further into it. But where's my fool? I have not seen him this two days.

Knight. Since my young lady's going into France, sir, the fool has much pined away.

Lear. No more of that; I have noted it well. Go you and tell my daughter I would speak with her.

[*Exit Knight*]

Go you, call here my Fool.

[*Exit an Attendant*]

But where's my fool? I have not seen him this two days.

[*Enter Oswald the Steward*]

O, you, sir, you! Come you here, sir. Who am I, sir?

Oswald. My lady's father.

Lear. "My lady's father"? My lord's knave! You whoreson dog! you slave! you cur!

Oswald. I am none of these, my lord; I beseech your pardon.

Lear. Do you bandy looks with me, you rascal?

[*Strikes him*]

Oswald. I'll not be struck, my lord.

Kent. Nor tripped neither, you base football player?

[*Trips up his heels*]

Lear. I thank you, fellow. You serve me, and I'll love you.

Kent. Come, sir, arise, away! I'll teach you differences. Away, away! If you will measure your lubber's length again, tarry; but away! Go to! Have you wisdom? So.

[*Pushes Oswald out*]

Lear. Now, my friendly knave, I thank you. There's earnest of your service.

[*Gives money*]

[*Enter Fool*]

Fool. Let me hire him too. Here's my coxcomb.

[*Offers Kent his cap*]

Lear. How now, my pretty knave? How do you?

Fool. Sirrah, you were best take my coxcomb.

Kent. Why, fool?

Fool. Why? For taking one's part that's out of favor. Nay, an you can not smile as the wind sits, you'll catch cold shortly. There, take my coxcomb! Why, this fellow has banished two of his daughters, and did the third a blessing against his will. If you follow him, you must needs wear my coxcomb.— How now, nuncle? Would I had two coxcombs and two daughters!

Lear. Why, my boy?

Fool. If I gave them all my living, I'd keep my coxcombs myself. There's mine! Beg another of your daughters.

I'll not be struck, my lord.

Lear. Take heed, sirrah— the whip.

Fool. Truth's a dog must to kennel; he must be whipped out, when Lady the brach may stand by the fire and stink.

Lear. A pestilent gall to me!

Fool. Sirrah, I'll teach you a speech.

Lear. Do.

Fool. Mark it, nuncle.

Have more than you show,
Speak less than you know,
Lend less than you owe,
Ride more than you go,
Learn more than you trow,
Set less than you throw;
Leave your drink and your whore,
And keep in-a-door,
And you shall have more
Than two tens to a score.

Kent. This is nothing, Fool.

Fool. Then it is like the breath of an unfeed lawyer— you gave me nothing for it. Can you make no use of nothing, nuncle?

Lear. Why, no, boy. Nothing can be made out of nothing.

Fool. [*to Kent*] Please tell him, so much the rent of his land comes to. He will not believe a Fool.

Lear. A bitter fool!

Fool. Do you know the difference, my boy, between a bitter fool and a sweet fool?

Lear. No, lad; teach me.

Fool. That lord that counselled you
To give away your land,
Come place him here by me—
Do you for him stand.
The sweet and bitter fool
Will presently appear;
The one in motley here,
The other found out there.

Lear. Do you call me fool, boy?

Fool. All your other titles you have given away; that you were born with.

Have more than you show,
Speak less than you know,
Lend less than you owe,

Kent. This is not altogether fool, my lord.

Fool. No, faith; lords and great men will not let me. If I had a monopoly out, they would have part on it. And ladies too, they will not let me have all the fool to myself; they'll be snatching. Give me an egg, nuncle, and I'll give you two crowns.

Lear. What two crowns shall they be?

Fool. Why, after I have cut the egg in the middle and eat up the meat, the two crowns of the egg. When you cloved your crown in the middle and gave away both parts, you bore your ass on your back over the dirt. You had little wit in your bald crown when you gave your golden one away. If I speak like myself in this, let him be whipped that first finds it so.

[*Sings*] Fools had never less grace in a year,
For wise men are grown foppish;
They know not how their wits to wear,
Their manners are so apish.

Lear. When were you wont to be so full of songs, sirrah?

Fool. I have used it, nuncle, ever since you made your daughters your mother; for when you gave them the rod, and put down your own breeches,

[Sings] Then they for sudden joy did weep,
And I for sorrow sung,
That such a king should play bo-peep
And go the fools among.

Please, nuncle, keep a schoolmaster that can teach your fool to lie. I would fain learn to lie.

Lear. An you lie, sirrah, we'll have you whipped.

Fool. I marvel what kin you and your daughters are. They'll have me whipped for speaking true; you'll have me whipped for lying; and sometimes I am whipped for holding my peace. I had rather be any kind of thing than a fool! And yet I would not be you, nuncle. You have pared your wit of both sides and left nothing in the middle. Here comes one of the parings.

Fools had never less grace in a year,

[*Enter Goneril*]

Lear. How now, daughter? What makes that frontlet on?
I think you are too much of late in the frown.

Fool. You were a pretty fellow when you had no need to care for her frowning. Now you are an O without a figure. I am better than you are now: I am a fool, you are nothing.
[*To Goneril*] Yes, forsooth, I will hold my tongue.
So your face bids me, though you say nothing.
Mum, mum!
He that keeps nor crust nor crumb,
Weary of all, shall want some.—

[*Points at Lear*]

That's a shealed peascod.

Goneril. Not only, sir, this your all-licensed fool,
But other of your insolent retinue
Do hourly carp and quarrel, breaking forth
In rank and not-to-be-endured riots. Sir,
I had thought, by making this well known unto you,
To have found a safe redress, but now grow fearful,
By what yourself, too, late have spoke and done,
That you protect this course, and put it on
By your allowance; which if you should, the fault
Would not scape censure, nor the redresses sleep,
Which, in the tender of a wholesome weal,
Might in their working do you that offence
Which else were shame, that then necessity
Must call discreet proceeding.

Fool. For you know, nuncle,
The hedge-sparrow fed the cuckoo so long
That it had its head bit off by its young.
So out went the candle, and we were left darkling.

Lear. Are you our daughter?

Goneril. Come, sir,
I would you would make use of that good wisdom
Whereof I know you are fraught, and put away
These dispositions that of late transform you
From what you rightly are.

Fool. May not an ass know when the cart draws the horse?
Whoop, Jug, I love you!

I am better than you are now: I am a fool, you are nothing.

Lear. Do any here know me? This is not Lear.
Does Lear walk thus? speak thus? Where are his eyes?
Either his notion weakens, his discernings
Are lethargied— Ha! waking? It's not so!
Who is it that can tell me who I am?

Fool. Lear's shadow.

Lear. I would learn that; for, by the marks of sovereignty,
Knowledge, and reason, I should be false persuaded
I had daughters.

Fool. Which they will make an obedient father.

Lear. Your name, fair gentlewoman?

Goneril. This admiration, sir, is much of the savor
Of other your new pranks. I do beseech you
To understand my purposes aright.
As you are old and reverend, you should be wise.
Here do you keep a hundred knights and squires;
Men so disordered, so deboshed, and bold
That this our court, infected with their manners,
Shows like a riotous inn. Epicurism and lust
Make it more like a tavern or a brothel
Than a graced palace. The shame itself does speak
For instant remedy. Be then desired
By her that else will take the thing she begs
A little to disquantity your train,
And the remainder that shall still depend
To be such men as may besort your age,
Which know themselves, and you.

Lear. Darkness and devils!
Saddle my horses! Call my train together!
Degenerate bastard, I'll not trouble you;
Yet have I left a daughter.

Goneril. You strike my people, and your disordered rabble
Make servants of their betters.

by the marks of sovereignty,
Knowledge, and reason, I should be false persuaded
I had daughters

[*Enter Albany*]

Lear. Woe that too late repents!— O, sir, are you come?
Is it your will? Speak, sir!— Prepare my horses.
Ingratitude, you marble-hearted fiend,
More hideous when you show you in a child
Than the sea-monster!

Albany. Pray, sir, be patient.

Lear. [*to Goneril*] Detested kite, you lie!
My train are men of choice and rarest parts,
That all particulars of duty know
And in the most exact regard support
The worships of their name.— O most small fault,
How ugly did you in Cordelia show!
Which, like an engine, wrenched my frame of nature
From the fixed place; drew from my heart all love
And added to the gall. O Lear, Lear, Lear!
Beat at this gate that let your folly in

[*Strikes his head*]

And your dear judgment out! Go, go, my people.

Albany. My lord, I am guiltless, as I am ignorant
Of what has moved you.

Lear. It may be so, my lord.
Hear, Nature, hear! dear goddess, hear!
Suspend your purpose, if you did intend
To make this creature fruitful.
Into her womb convey sterility;
Dry up in her the organs of increase;
And from her derogate body never spring
A babe to honor her! If she must teem,
Create her child of spleen, that it may live
And be a thwart disnatured torment to her.
Let it stamp wrinkles in her brow of youth,
With cadent tears fret channels in her cheeks,
Turn all her mother's pains and benefits
To laughter and contempt, that she may feel
How sharper than a serpent's tooth it is
To have a thankless child! Away, away!

[*Exit Lear*]

Albany. Now, gods that we adore, whereof comes this?

Goneril. Never afflict yourself to know the cause;
But let his disposition have that scope
That dotage gives it.

Hear, Nature, hear! dear goddess, hear!
Suspend your purpose, if you did intend
To make this creature fruitful

[*Re-enter Lear*]

Lear. What, fifty of my followers at a clap?
Within a fortnight?

Albany. What's the matter, sir?

Lear. I'll tell you. [*To Goneril*] Life and death! I am ashamed
That you have power to shake my manhood thus;
That these hot tears, which break from me perforce,
Should make you worth them. Blasts and fogs upon you!
The untented woundings of a father's curse
Pierce every sense about you!— Old fond eyes,
Beweep this cause again, I'll pluck you out,
And cast you, with the waters that you lose,
To temper clay. Yea, is it come to this?
Let it be so. Yet have I left a daughter,
Who I am sure is kind and comfortable.
When she shall hear this of you, with her nails
She'll flay your wolvish visage. You shall find
That I'll resume the shape which you do think
I have cast off forever; you shall, I warrant you.

[*Exeunt Lear, Kent, and Attendants*]

Goneril. Do you mark that, my lord?

Albany. I cannot be so partial, Goneril,
To the great love I bear you —

Goneril. Pray you, content.— What, Oswald, ho!
[*To the Fool*] You, sir, more knave than fool, after your master!

Fool. Nuncle Lear, nuncle Lear, tarry! Take the fool with you.

A fox when one has caught her,
And such a daughter,
Should sure to the slaughter,
If my cap would buy a halter.
So the fool follows after.

[*Exit Fool*]

I am ashamed
That you have power to shake my manhood thus

Goneril. This man has had good counsel! A hundred knights?
It's politic and safe to let him keep
At point a hundred knights; yes, that on every dream,
Each buzz, each fancy, each complaint, dislike,
He may enguard his dotage with their powers
And hold our lives in mercy.— Oswald, I say!

Albany. Well, you may fear too far.

Goneril. Safer than trust too far.
Let me still take away the harms I fear,
Not fear still to be taken. I know his heart.
What he has uttered I have writ my sister.
If she sustain him and his hundred knights,
When I have showed the unfitness—

[*Enter Oswald the Steward*]

How now, Oswald?
What, have you writ that letter to my sister?

Oswald. Yes, madam.

Goneril. Take you some company, and away to horse!
Inform her full of my particular fear,
And thereto add such reasons of your own
As may compact it more. Get you gone,
And hasten your return.

[*Exit Oswald*]

No, no, my lord!
This milky gentleness and course of yours,
Though I condemn it not, yet, under pardon,
You are much more at task for want of wisdom
Than praised for harmful mildness.

Albany. How far your eyes may pierce I cannot tell.
Striving to better, oft we mar what's well.

Goneril. Nay then—

Albany. Well, well; the event.

[*Exeunt*]

Inform her full of my particular fear,
And thereto add such reasons of your own

[Court before the Duke of Albany's Palace]

[Enter Lear, Kent, and Fool]

Lear. Go you before to Gloucester with these letters. Acquaint my daughter no further with anything you know than comes from her demand out of the letter. If your diligence be not speedy, I shall be there afore you.

Kent. I will not sleep, my lord, till I have delivered your letter.

[Exit Kent]

Fool. If a man's brains were in his heels, were it not in danger of kibes?

Lear. Ay, boy.

Fool. Then please be merry. Your wit shall never go slip-shod.

Lear. Ha, ha, ha!

Fool. Shall see your other daughter will use you kindly; for though she's as like this as a crab's like an apple, yet I can tell what I can tell.

Lear. What can tell, boy?

Fool. She'll taste as like this as a crab does to a crab. You can tell why one's nose stands in the middle on its face?

Lear. No.

Fool. Why, to keep one's eyes of either side of its nose, that what a man cannot smell out, he may spy into.

Lear. I did her wrong.

Fool. Can tell how an oyster makes his shell?

Lear. No.

Fool. Nor I neither; but I can tell why a snail has a house.

Lear. Why?

Fool. Why, to put his head in; not to give it away to his daughters, and leave his horns without a case.

Lear. I will forget my nature. So kind a father!— Be my horses ready?

Fool. Your asses are gone about 'em. The reason why the seven stars are no more than seven is a pretty reason.

Lear. Because they are not eight?

Fool. Yes indeed. You would make a good fool.

Lear. To take it again perforce! Monster ingratitude!

Fool. If you were my fool, nuncle, I'd have you beaten for being old before your time.

Lear. How's that?

Fool. You should not have been old till you had been wise.

If a man's brains were in his heels, were it not in danger of kibes?

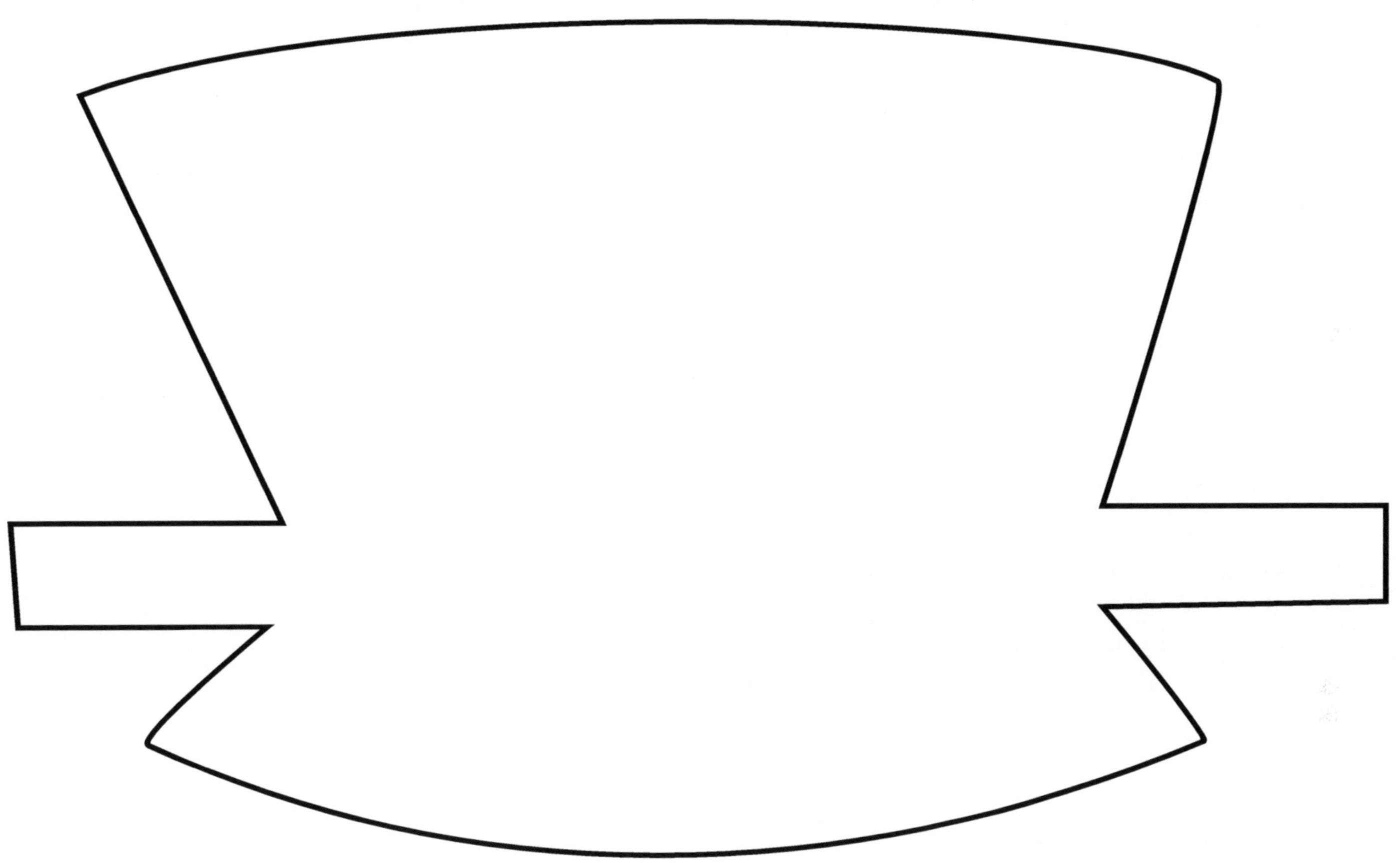

Lear. O, let me not be mad, not mad, sweet heaven!
Keep me in temper; I would not be mad!

[*Enter a Gentleman*]

How now? Are the horses ready?

Gentleman. Ready, my lord.

Lear. Come, boy.

Fool. She that's a maid now, and laughs at my departure,
Shall not be a maid long, unless things be cut shorter.

[*Exeunt*]

Act Two

1

[A court within the Castle of the Earl of Gloucester]

[Enter Edmund *the Bastard and Curan, meeting]*

Edmund. Save you, Curan.

Curan. And you, sir. I have been with your father, and given him notice that the Duke of Cornwall and Regan his Duchess will be here with him this night.

Edmund. How comes that?

Curan. Nay, I know not. You have heard of the news abroad— I mean the whispered ones, for they are yet but ear-kissing arguments?

Edmund. Not I. Pray you, what are they?

Curan. Have you heard of no likely wars toward between the two Dukes of Cornwall and Albany?

Edmund. Not a word.

Curan. You may do, then, in time. Fare you well, sir.

[Exit Curan]

Edmund. The Duke be here tonight? The better! best!
This weaves itself perforce into my business.
My father has set guard to take my brother;
And I have one thing, of a queasy question,
Which I must act. Briefness and fortune, work!
Brother, a word! Descend! Brother, I say!

[Enter Edgar]

My father watches. O sir, fly this place!
Intelligence is given where you are hid.
You have now the good advantage of the night.
Have you not spoken against the Duke of Cornwall?
He's coming here; now, in the night, in the haste,
And Regan with him. Have you nothing said
Upon his party against the Duke of Albany?
Advise yourself.

Edgar. I am sure on it, not a word.

The Duke be here tonight? The better! best!
This weaves itself perforce into my business.

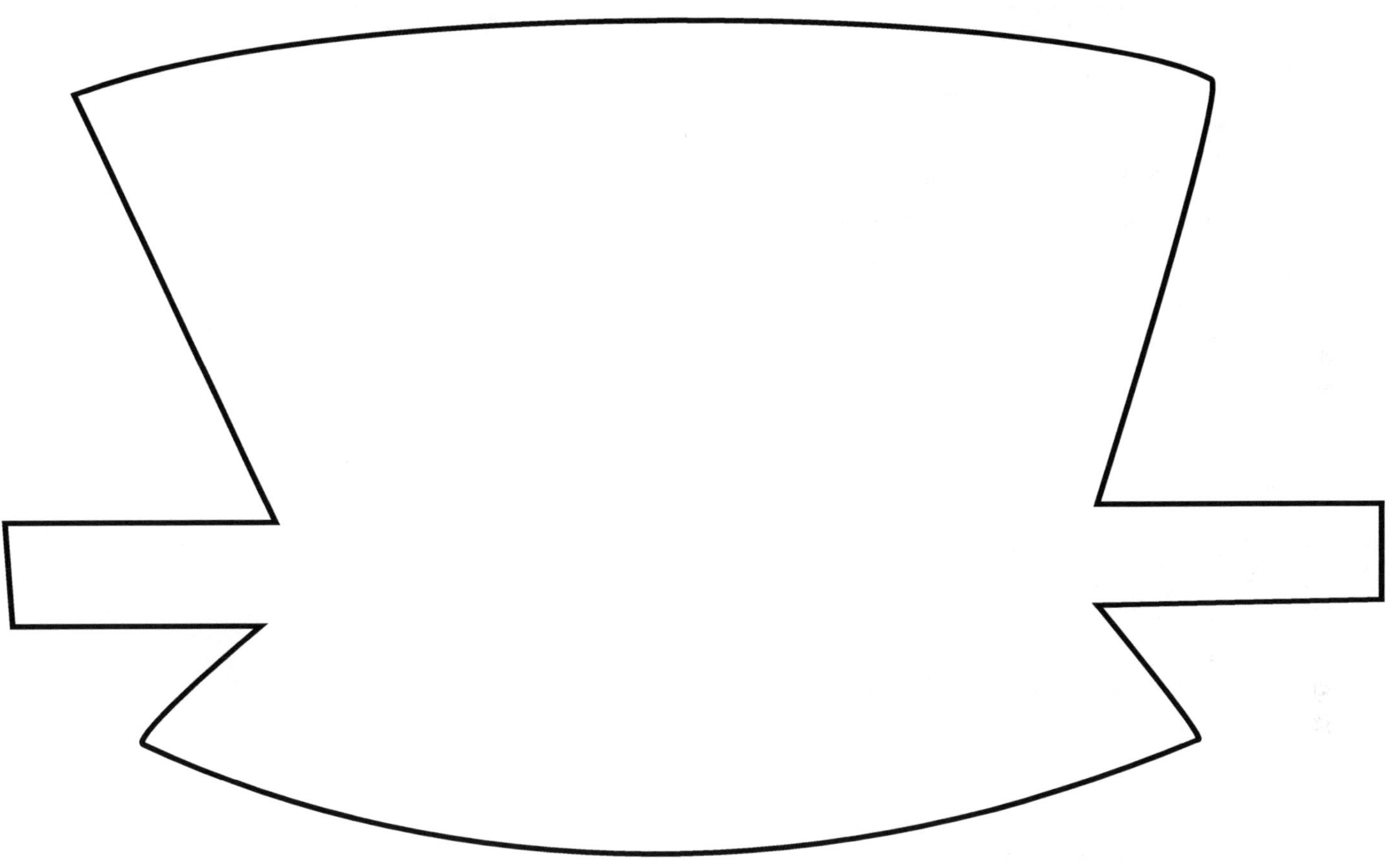

Edmund. I hear my father coming. Pardon me!
In cunning I must draw my sword upon you.
Draw, seem to defend yourself; now quit you well.—
Yield! Come before my father. Light, ho, here!
Fly, brother.— Torches, torches!— So farewell.

[*Exit Edgar*]

Edmund. Some blood drawn on me would beget opinion
Of my more fierce endeavor.

[*Stabs his arm.*]

I have seen drunkards
Do more than this in sport.— Father, father!—
Stop, stop! No help?

[*Enter Gloucester, and Servants with torches*]

Gloucester. Now, Edmund, where's the villain?

Edmund. Here stood he in the dark, his sharp sword out,
Mumbling of wicked charms, conjuring the moon
To stand his auspicious mistress.

Gloucester. But where is he?

Edmund. Look, sir, I bleed.

Gloucester. Where is the villain, Edmund?

Edmund. Fled this way, sir. When by no means he could—
Gloucester. Pursue him, ho! Go after.

[*Exeunt some Servants*]

By no means what?

Edmund. Persuade me to the murder of your lordship;
But that I told him the revenging gods
Against parricides did all their thunders bend;
Spoke with how manifold and strong a bond
The child was bound to the father— sir, in fine,
Seeing how loathly opposite I stood
To his unnatural purpose, in fell motion
With his prepared sword he charges home
My unprovided body, lanched my arm;
But when he saw my best alarumed spirits,
Bold in the quarrel's right, roused to the encounter,
Or whether gasted by the noise I made,
Full suddenly he fled.

Gloucester. Let him fly far.
Not in this land shall he remain uncaught;
And found— dispatch. The noble Duke my master,
My worthy arch and patron, comes tonight.
By his authority I will proclaim it
That he which find him shall deserve our thanks,
Bringing the murderous caitiff to the stake;
He that conceals him, death.

Now, Edmund, where's the villain?

Edmund. When I dissuaded him from his intent
And found him pight to do it, with cursed speech
I threatened to discover him. He replied,
"You unpossessing bastard, do you think,
If I would stand against you, would the reposal
Of any trust, virtue, or worth in you
Make your words faithed? No. *What I should deny*
(As this I would; ay, though you did produce
My very character), I'd turn it all
To your suggestion, plot, and damned practice;
And you must make a dullard of the world,
If they not thought the profits of my death
Were very pregnant and potential spurs
To make you seek it."

Gloucester. Strong and fastened villain!
Would he deny his letter? I never got him.

[*Trumpet within*]

Hark, the Duke's trumpets! I know not why he comes.
All ports I'll bar; the villain shall not scape;
The Duke must grant me that. Besides, his picture
I will send far and near, that all the kingdom
May have due note of him, and of my land,
Loyal and natural boy, I'll work the means
To make you capable

[*Enter Cornwall, Regan, and Attendants*]

Cornwall. How now, my noble friend? Since I came here
(Which I can call but now) I have heard strange news.

Regan. If it be true, all vengeance comes too short
Which can pursue the offender. How does, my lord?

Gloucester. O madam, my old heart is cracked, it's cracked!

Regan. What, did my father's godson seek your life?
He whom my father named? Your Edgar?

Gloucester. O lady, lady, shame would have it hid!

Regan. Was he not companion with the riotous knights
That tend upon my father?

Gloucester. I know not, madam. It's too bad, too bad!

Edmund. Yes, madam, he was of that consort.

And you must make a dullard of the world,
If they not thought the profits of my death
Were very pregnant and potential spurs

Regan. No marvel then though he were ill affected.
It's they have put him on the old man's death,
To have the expense and waste of his revenues.
I have this present evening from my sister
Been well informed of them, and with such cautions
That, if they come to sojourn at my house,
I'll not be there.

Cornwall. Nor I, assure you, Regan.
Edmund, I hear that you have shown your father
A childlike office.

Edmund. It was my duty, sir.

Gloucester. He did bewray his practice, and received
This hurt you see, striving to apprehend him.

Cornwall. Is he pursued?

Gloucester. Ay, my good lord.

Cornwall. If he be taken, he shall never more
Be feared of doing harm. Make your own purpose,
How in my strength you please. For you, Edmund,
Whose virtue and obedience does this instant
So much commend itself, you shall be ours.
Natures of such deep trust we shall much need;
You we first seize on.

Edmund. I shall serve you, sir,
Truly, however else.

Gloucester. For him I thank your Grace.

Cornwall. You know not why we came to visit you—

Regan. Thus out of season, threading dark-eyed night.
Occasions, noble Gloucester, of some poise,
Wherein we must have use of your advice.
Our father he has writ, so has our sister,
Of differences, which I best thought it fit
To answer from our home. The several messengers
From hence attend dispatch. Our good old friend,
Lay comforts to your bosom, and bestow
Your needful counsel to our business,
Which craves the instant use.

Gloucester. I serve you, madam.
Your Graces are right welcome.

[*Exeunt. Flourish*]

Natures of such deep trust we shall much need

2

[*Before Gloucester's Castle*]

[*Enter Kent and Oswald the Steward, severally*]

Oswald. Good dawning to you, friend. Are of this house?

Kent. Ay.

Oswald. Where may we set our horses?

Kent. In the mire.

Oswald. Please, if you love me, tell me.

Kent. I love you not.

Oswald. Why then, I care not for you.

Kent. If I had you in Lipsbury Pinfold, I would make you care for me.

Oswald. Why do you use me thus? I know you not.

Kent. Fellow, I know you.

Oswald. What do you know me for?

Kent. A knave; a rascal; an eater of broken meats; a base, proud, shallow, beggarly, three-suited, hundred-pound, filthy, worsted-stocking knave; a lily-livered, action-taking, whoreson, glass-gazing, superserviceable, finical rogue; one-trunk-inheriting slave; one that would be a bawd in way of good service, and are nothing but the composition of a knave, beggar, coward, pander, and the son and heir of a mongrel bitch; one whom I will beat into clamorous whining, if you deny the least syllable of your addition.

Oswald. Why, what a monstrous fellow are you, thus to rail on one that's neither known of you nor knows you!

Kent. What a brazen-faced varlet are you, to deny you know me! Is it two days ago since I beat you and tripped up your heels before the King?

[*Draws his sword*]

Draw, you rogue! for, though it be night, yet the moon shines. I'll make a sop of the moonshine of you. Draw, you whoreson cullionly barbermonger! Draw!

Oswald. Away! I have nothing to do with you.

Kent. Draw, you rascal! You come with letters against the King, and take vanity the puppet's part against the royalty of her father. Draw, you rogue, or I'll so carbonado your shanks! Draw, you rascal! Come your ways!

A knave; a rascal; an eater of broken meats; a base, proud, shallow, beggarly, three-suited, hundred-pound, filthy, worsted-stocking knave

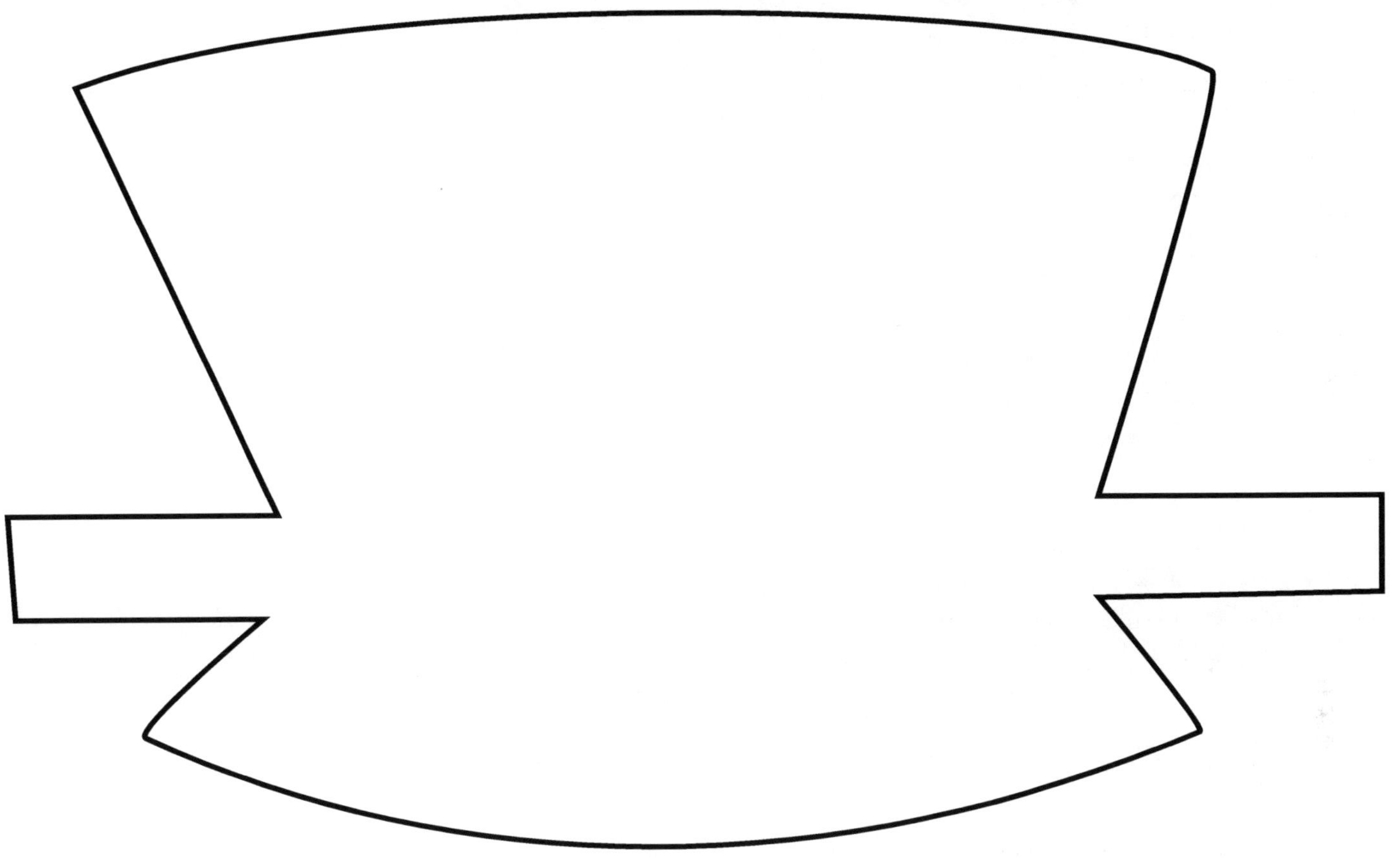

Oswald. Help, ho! murder! help!

Kent. Strike, you slave! Stand, rogue! Stand, you neat slave! Strike!

[*Beats him*]

Oswald. Help, ho! murder! murder!

[*Enter Edmund, with his rapier drawn, Gloucester, Cornwall, Regan, Servants*]

Edmund. How now? What's the matter?

[*Parts them*]

Kent. With you, goodman boy, if you please! Come, I'll flesh you!
Come on, young master!

Gloucester. Weapons? arms? What's the matter here?

Cornwall. Keep peace, upon your lives!
He dies that strikes again. What is the matter?

Regan. The messengers from our sister and the King

Cornwall. What is your difference? Speak.

Oswald. I am scarce in breath, my lord.

Kent. No marvel, you have so bestirred your valor. You cowardly rascal, nature disclaims in you; a tailor made you.

Cornwall. You are a strange fellow. A tailor make a man?

Kent. Ay, a tailor, sir. A stonecutter or a painter could not have made him so ill, though he had been but two hours at the trade.

Cornwall. Speak yet, how grew your quarrel?

Oswald. This ancient ruffian, sir, whose life I have spared
At suit of his grey beard—

Kent. You whoreson zed! you unnecessary letter! My lord, if you'll give me leave, I will tread this unbolted villain into mortar and daub the walls of a jakes with him. "Spare my grey beard," you wagtail?

Cornwall. Peace, sirrah!
You beastly knave, know you no reverence?

Kent. Yes, sir, but anger has a privilege.

Cornwall. Why are you angry?

Kent. That such a slave as this should wear a sword,
Who wears no honesty. Such smiling rogues as these,
Like rats, oft bite the holy cords atwain
Which are too intrinse to unloose; smooth every passion
That in the natures of their lords rebel,
Bring oil to fire, snow to their colder moods;
Renege, affirm, and turn their halcyon beaks
With every gale and vary of their masters,
Knowing naught (like dogs) but following.
A plague upon your epileptic visage!
Smile you my speeches, as I were a fool?
Goose, an I had you upon Sarum Plain,
I'd drive you cackling home to Camelot.

Speak yet, how grew your quarrel?

Cornwall. What, are you mad, old fellow?

Gloucester. How fell you out? Say that.

Kent. No contraries hold more antipathy
Than I and such a knave.

Cornwall. Why do you call him knave? What is his fault?

Kent. His countenance likes me not.

Cornwall. No more perchance does mine, or his, or hers.

Kent. Sir, it is my occupation to be plain.
I have seen better faces in my time
Than stands on any shoulder that I see
Before me at this instant.

Cornwall. This is some fellow
Who, having been praised for bluntness, does affect
A saucy roughness, and constrains the garb
Quite from his nature. He cannot flatter, he!
An honest mind and plain— he must speak truth!
An they will take it, so; if not, he's plain.
These kind of knaves I know which in this plainness
Harbor more craft and more corrupter ends
Than twenty silly-ducking observants
That stretch their duties nicely.

Kent. Sir, in good faith, in sincere verity,
Under the allowance of your great aspect,
Whose influence, like the wreath of radiant fire
On flickering Phoebus' front—

Cornwall. What mean by this?

Kent. To go out of my dialect, which you discommend so much. I know, sir, I am no flatterer. He that beguiled you in a
plain accent was a plain knave, which, for my part, I will not be, though I should win your displeasure to entreat me to it.

Cornwall. What was the offence you gave him?

Oswald. I never gave him any.
It pleased the King his master very late
To strike at me, upon his misconstruction;
When he, conjunct, and flattering his displeasure,
Tripped me behind; being down, insulted, railed
And put upon him such a deal of man
That worthied him, got praises of the King
For him attempting who was self-subdued;
And, in the fleshment of this dread exploit,
Drew on me here again.

Kent. None of these rogues and cowards
But Ajax is their Fool.

He cannot flatter, he!
An honest mind and plain— he must speak truth!

Cornwall. Fetch forth the stocks!
You stubborn ancient knave, you reverent braggart,
We'll teach you—

Kent. Sir, I am too old to learn.
Call not your stocks for me. I serve the King;
On whose employment I was sent to you.
You shall do small respect, show too bold malice
Against the grace and person of my master,
Stocking his messenger.

Cornwall. Fetch forth the stocks! As I have life and
honor,
There shall he sit till noon.

Regan. Till noon? Till night, my lord, and all night too!

Kent. Why, madam, if I were your father's dog,
You should not use me so.

Regan. Sir, being his knave, I will.

Cornwall. This is a fellow of the selfsame color
Our sister speaks of. Come, bring away the stocks!
Stocks brought out.

Gloucester. Let me beseech your Grace not to do so.
His fault is much, and the good King his master
Will check him for it. Your purposed low correction
Is such as basest and contemnedest wretches
For pilferings and most common trespasses
Are punished with. The King must take it ill
That he, so slightly valued in his messenger,
Should have him thus restrained.

Cornwall. I'll answer that.

Regan. My sister may receive it much more worse,
To have her gentleman abused, assaulted,
For following her affairs. Put in his legs.—

[*Kent is put in the stocks*]

Come, my good lord, away.

[*Exeunt all but Gloucester and Kent*]

. Call not your stocks for me. I serve the King

Gloucester. I am sorry for you, friend. It's the Duke's pleasure,
Whose disposition, all the world well knows,
Will not be rubbed nor stopped. I'll entreat for you.

Kent. Pray do not, sir. I have watched and travelled hard.
Some time I shall sleep out, the rest I'll whistle.
A good man's fortune may grow out at heels.
Give you good morrow!

Gloucester. The Duke's to blame in this; it will be ill taken.

[*Exit Gloucester*]

Kent. Good King, that must approve the common saw,
You out of heaven's benediction come
To the warm sun!
Approach, you beacon to this under globe,
That by your comfortable beams I may
Peruse this letter. Nothing almost sees miracles
But misery. I know it is from Cordelia,
Who has most fortunately been informed
Of my obscured course— and [*reads*] "shall find time
From this enormous state, seeking to give
Losses their remedies"— All weary and overwatched,
Take vantage, heavy eyes, not to behold
This shameful lodging.
Fortune, good night; smile once more, turn your wheel.

[*Sleep*]

Take vantage, heavy eyes, not to behold
This shameful lodging.

3

[*The open country*]

[*Enter Edgar*]

Edgar. I heard myself proclaimed,
And by the happy hollow of a tree
Escaped the hunt. No port is free, no place
That guard and most unusual vigilance
Does not attend my taking. While I may scape,
I will preserve myself; and am bethought
To take the basest and most poorest shape
That ever penury, in contempt of man,
Brought near to beast. My face I'll grime with filth,
Blanket my loins, elf all my hair in knots,
And with presented nakedness outface
The winds and persecutions of the sky.
The country gives me proof and precedent
Of Bedlam beggars, who, with roaring voices,
Strike in their numbed and mortified bare arms
Pins, wooden pricks, nails, sprigs of rosemary;
And with this horrible object, from low farms,
Poor pelting villages, sheepcotes, and mills,
Sometime with lunatic bans, sometime with prayers,
Enforce their charity. "Poor Turlygod! poor Tom!'
That's something yet! Edgar I nothing am.

[*Exit*]

am bethought
To take the basest and most poorest shape
That ever penury, in contempt of man,

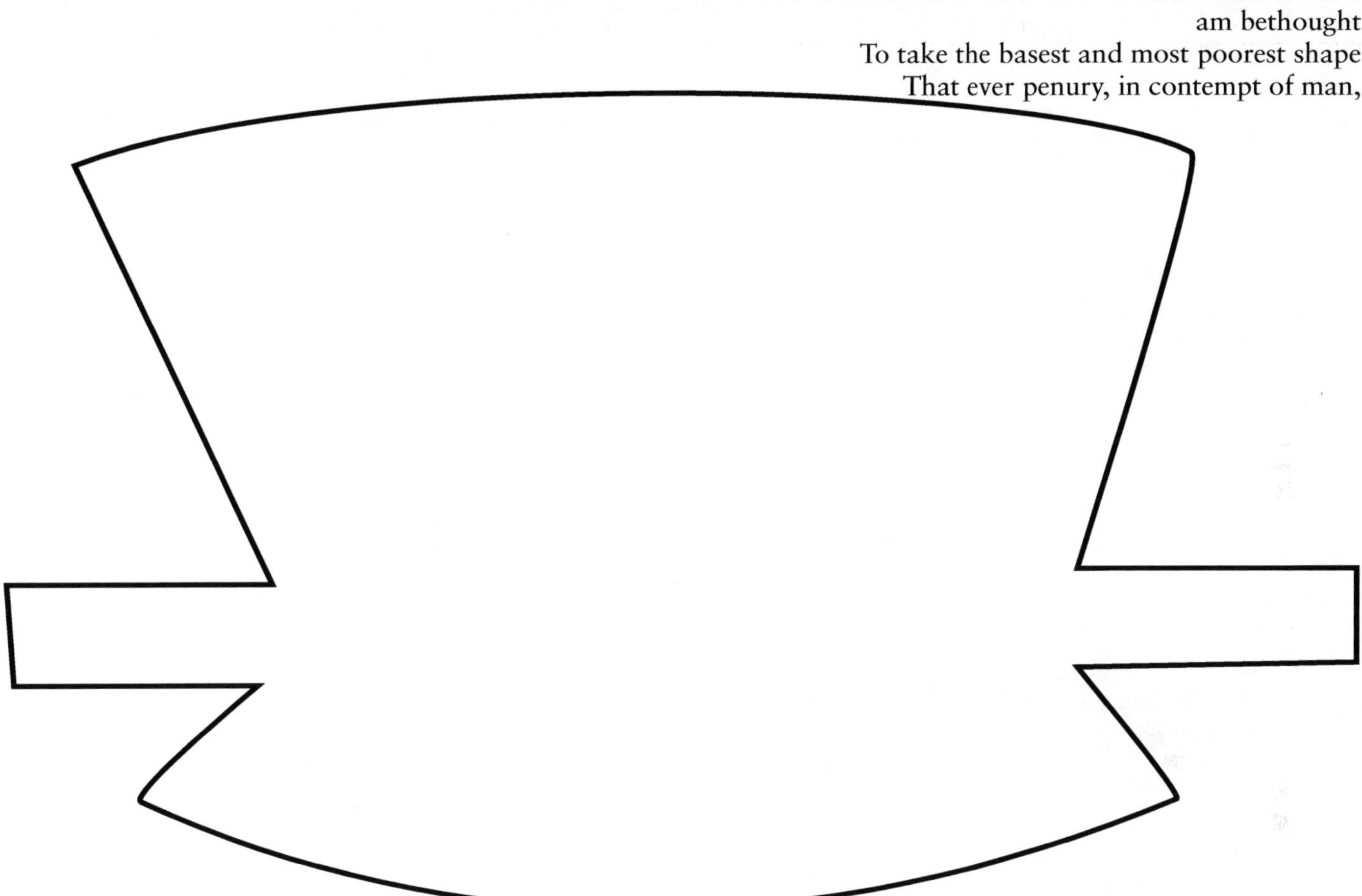

4

[Before Gloucester's Castle; Kent in the stocks]

[Enter Lear, Fool, and Gentleman]

Lear. It's strange that they should so depart from home,
And not send back my messenger.

Gentleman. As I learned,
The night before there was no purpose in them
Of this remove.

Kent. Hail to you, noble master!

Lear. Ha!
Make you this shame your pastime?

Kent. No, my lord.

Fool. Ha, ha! look! he wears cruel garters. Horses are tied by the head, dogs and bears by the neck, monkeys by the loins, and men by the legs. When a man's over-lusty at legs, then he wears wooden nether-stocks.

Lear. What's he that has so much your place mistook
To set you here?

Kent. It is both he and she—
Your son and daughter.

Lear. No.

Kent. Yes.

Lear. No, I say.

Kent. I say yea.

Lear. No, no, they would not!

Kent. Yes, they have.

Lear. By Jupiter, I swear no!

Kent. By Juno, I swear ay!

Lear. They dare not do it;
They would not, could not do it. It's worse than murder
To do upon respect such violent outrage.
Resolve me with all modest haste which way
You might deserve or they impose this usage,
Coming from us.

Ha, ha! look! he wears cruel garters

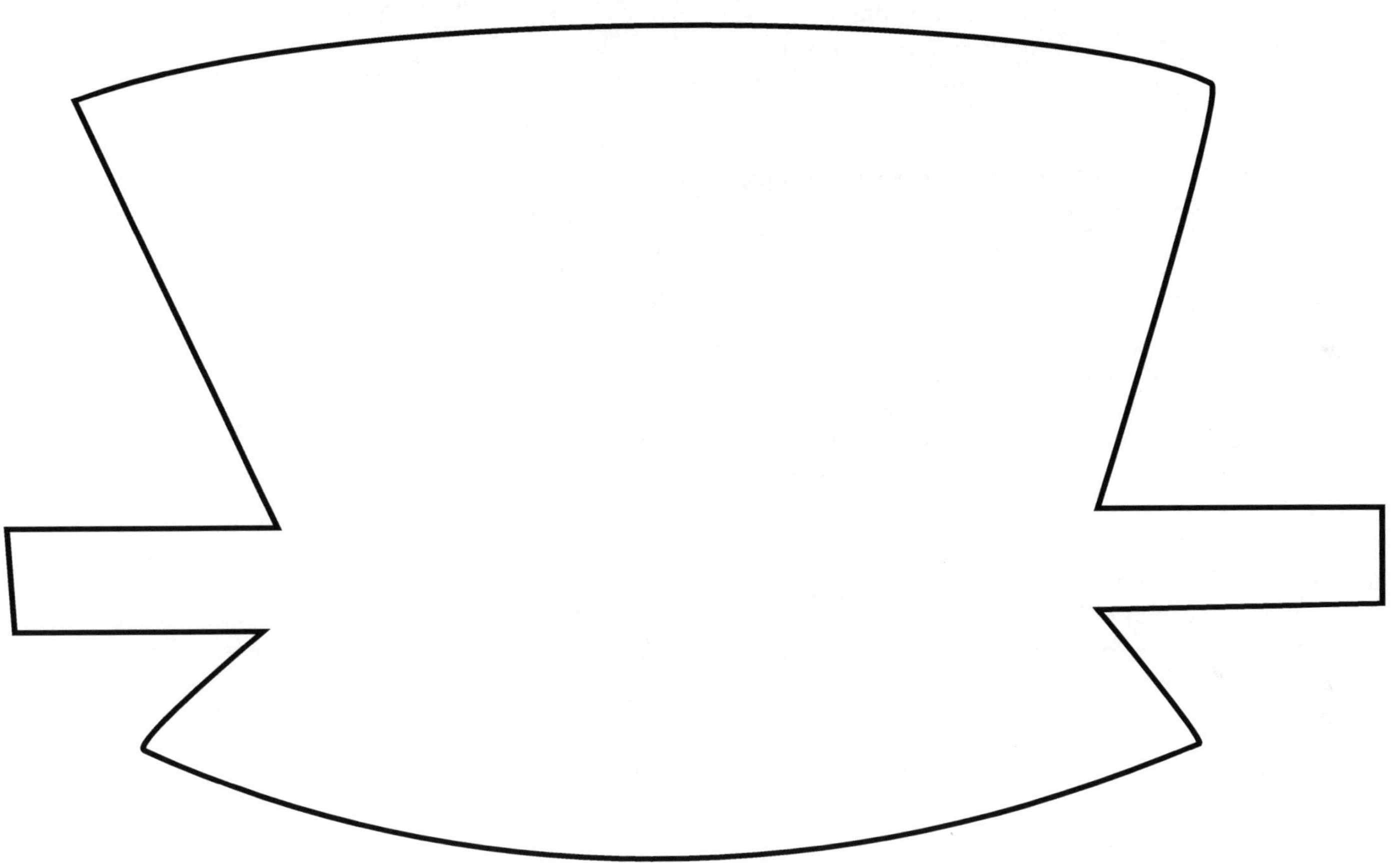

Kent. My lord, when at their home
I did commend your Highness' letters to them,
Before I was risen from the place that showed
My duty kneeling, came there a reeking post,
Stewed in his haste, half breathless, panting forth
From Goneril his mistress salutations;
Delivered letters, spite of intermission,
Which presently they read; on whose contents,
They summoned up their meiny, straight took horse,
Commanded me to follow and attend
The leisure of their answer, gave me cold looks,
And meeting here the other messenger,
Whose welcome I perceived had poisoned mine—
Being the very fellow which of late
Displayed so saucily against your Highness—
Having more man than wit about me, drew.
He raised the house with loud and coward cries.
Your son and daughter found this trespass worth
The shame which here it suffers.

Fool. Winter's not gone yet, if the wild geese fly that way.
Fathers that wear rags
Do make their children blind;
But fathers that bear bags
Shall see their children kind.
Fortune, that arrant whore,
Never turns the key to the poor.
But for all this, you shall have as many dolors for
your
daughters as you can tell in a year.

Lear. O, how this mother swells up toward my heart!
Hysterica passio! Down, you climbing sorrow!
Your element's below! Where is this daughter?

Kent. With the Earl, sir, here within.

Lear. Follow me not;
Stay here.

[*Exit Lear*]

Fathers that wear rags
Do make their children blind;
But fathers that bear bags
Shall see their children kind.

Gentleman. Made you no more offence but what you speak of?

Kent. None.
How chance the King comes with so small a number?

Fool. If you had been set in the stocks for that question, you'd well deserved it.

Kent. Why, fool?

Fool. We'll set you to school to an ant, to teach you there's no laboring in the winter. All that follow their noses are led by their eyes but blind men, and there's not a nose among twenty but can smell him that's stinking. Let go your hold when a great wheel runs down a hill, lest it break your neck with following it; but the great one that goes upward, let him draw you after.
When a wise man gives you better counsel, give me mine again. I would have none but knaves follow it, since a fool gives it.

That sir which serves and seeks for gain,
And follows but for form,
Will pack when it begins to rain
And leave you in the storm.
But I will tarry; the fool will stay,
And let the wise man fly.
The knave turns fool that runs away;
The fool no knave, perdy.

Kent. Where learned you this, fool?

Fool. Not in the stocks, fool.

That sir which serves and seeks for gain,
And follows but for form,
Will pack when it begins to rain
And leave you in the storm.

[*Enter Lear and Gloucester*]

Lear. Deny to speak with me? They are sick? They are weary?
They have travelled all the night? Mere fetches—
The images of revolt and flying off!
Fetch me a better answer.

Gloucester. My dear lord,
You know the fiery quality of the Duke,
How unremovable and fixed he is
In his own course.

Lear. Vengeance! plague! death! confusion!
Fiery? What quality? Why, Gloucester, Gloucester,
I'd speak with the Duke of Cornwall and his wife.

Gloucester. Well, my good lord, I have informed them so.

Lear. Informed them? Do you understand me, man?

Gloucester. Ay, my good lord.

Lear. The King would speak with Cornwall; the dear father
Would with his daughter speak, commands her service.
Are they informed of this? My breath and blood!
Fiery? the fiery Duke? Tell the hot Duke that—
No, but not yet! Maybe he is not well.
Infirmity does still neglect all office
Whereto our health is bound. We are not ourselves
When nature, being oppressed, commands the mind
To suffer with the body. I'll forbear;
And am fallen out with my more headier will,
To take the indisposed and sickly fit
For the sound man— Death on my state! Wherefore
Should be sit here? This act persuades me
That this remotion of the Duke and her
Is practice only. Give me my servant forth.
Go tell the Duke and his wife I'd speak with them—
Now, presently. Bid them come forth and hear me,
Or at their chamber door I'll beat the drum
Till it cry sleep to death.

Gloucester. I would have all well between you.

[*Exit Gloucester*]

The King would speak with Cornwall; the dear father
Would with his daughter speak, commands her service.

Lear. O me, my heart, my rising heart! But down!

Fool. Cry to it, nuncle, as the cockney did to the eels when she put 'em in the paste alive. She knapped 'em of the coxcombs with a stick and cried "Down, wantons, down!" It was her brother that, in pure kindness to his horse, buttered his hay.

[*Enter Cornwall, Regan, Gloucester, Servants*]

Lear. Good morrow to you both.

Cornwall. Hail to your Grace!
Kent here set at liberty.

Regan. I am glad to see your Highness.

Lear. Regan, I think you are; I know what reason
I have to think so. If you should not be glad,
I would divorce me from your mother's tomb,
Sepulchring an adultress. [*To Kent*] O, are you free?
Some other time for that— Beloved Regan,
Your sister's naught. O Regan, she has tied
Sharp-toothed unkindness, like a vulture, here!

[*Lays his hand on his heart*]

I can scarce speak to you. You'll not believe
With how depraved a quality— O Regan!

Regan. I pray you, sir, take patience. I have hope
You less know how to value her desert
Than she to scant her duty.

Lear. Say, how is that?

Regan. I cannot think my sister in the least
Would fail her obligation. If, sir, perchance
She have restrained the riots of your followers,
It's on such ground, and to such wholesome end,
As clears her from all blame.

Lear. My curses on her!

Regan. O, sir, you are old!
Nature in you stands on the very verge
Of her confine. You should be ruled, and led
By some discretion that discerns your state
Better than you yourself. Therefore I pray you
That to our sister you do make return;
Say you have wronged her, sir.

Lear. Ask her forgiveness?
Do you but mark how this becomes the house:
"Dear daughter, I confess that I am old.

[*Kneels*]

Age is unnecessary. On my knees I beg
That you'll vouchsafe me raiment, bed, and food."

I cannot think my sister in the least
Would fail her obligation

Regan. Good sir, no more! These are unsightly tricks.
Return you to my sister.

Lear. [*rises*] Never, Regan!
She has abated me of half my train;
Looked black upon me; struck me with her tongue,
Most serpent-like, upon the very heart.
All the stored vengeances of heaven fall
On her ingrateful top! Strike her young bones,
You taking airs, with lameness!

Cornwall. Fie, sir, fie!

Lear. You nimble lightnings, dart your blinding flames
Into her scornful eyes! Infect her beauty,
You fen-sucked fogs, drawn by the powerful sun,
To fall and blast her pride!

Regan. O the blessed gods! so will you wish on me
When the rash mood is on.

Lear. No, Regan, you shall never have my curse.
Your tender-hefted nature shall not give
You over to harshness. Her eyes are fierce; but yours
Do comfort, and not burn. It's not in you
To grudge my pleasures, to cut off my train,
To bandy hasty words, to scant my sizes,
And, in conclusion, to oppose the bolt
Against my coming in. You better know
The offices of nature, bond of childhood,
Effects of courtesy, dues of gratitude.
Your half of the kingdom have you not forgot,
Wherein I you endowed.

Regan. Good sir, to the purpose.

[*Tucket within*]

Lear. Who put my man in the stocks?

Cornwall. What trumpet's that?

Regan. I know it— my sister's. This approves her letter,
That she would soon be here.

[*Enter Oswald the Steward*]

Is your lady come.

Lear. This is a slave, whose easy-borrowed pride
Dwells in the fickle grace of her he follows.
Out, varlet, from my sight!

Cornwall. What means your Grace?

She has abated me of half my train;
Looked black upon me; struck me with her tongue

[*Enter Goneril*]

Lear. Who stocked my servant? Regan, I have good hope
You did not know on it— Who comes here? O heavens!
If you do love old men, if your sweet sway
Allow obedience— if yourselves are old,
Make it your cause! Send down, and take my part!
[*To Goneril*] Are not ashamed to look upon this beard?—
O Regan, will you take her by the hand?

Goneril. Why not by the hand, sir? How have I offended?
All's not offence that indiscretion finds
And dotage terms so.

Lear. O sides, you are too tough!
Will you yet hold? How came my man in the stocks?

Cornwall. I set him there, sir; but his own disorders
Deserved much less advancement.

Lear. You? Did you?

Regan. I pray you, father, being weak, seem so.
If, till the expiration of your month,
You will return and sojourn with my sister,
Dismissing half your train, come then to me.
I am now from home, and out of that provision
Which shall be needful for your entertainment.

Lear. Return to her, and fifty men dismissed?
No, rather I abjure all roofs, and choose
To wage against the enmity of the air,
To be a comrade with the wolf and owl—
Necessity's sharp pinch! Return with her?
Why, the hot-blooded France, that dowerless took
Our youngest born, I could as well be brought
To knee his throne, and, squire-like, pension beg
To keep base life afoot. Return with her?
Persuade me rather to be slave and sumpter
To this detested groom.

[*Points at Oswald*]

Goneril. At your choice, sir.

I pray you, father, being weak, seem so.

Lear. I pray, daughter, do not make me mad.
I will not trouble you, my child; farewell.
We'll no more meet, no more see one another.
But yet you are my flesh, my blood, my daughter;
Or rather a disease that's in my flesh,
Which I must needs call mine. You are a boil,
A plague sore, an embossed carbuncle
In my corrupted blood. But I'll not chide you.
Let shame come when it will, I do not call it.
I do not bid the Thunder-bearer shoot
Nor tell tales of you to high-judging Jove.
Mend when you can; be better at your leisure;
I can be patient, I can stay with Regan,
I and my hundred knights.

Regan. Not altogether so.
I looked not for you yet, nor am provided
For your fit welcome. Give ear, sir, to my sister;
For those that mingle reason with your passion
Must be content to think you old, and so—
But she knows what she does.

Lear. Is this well spoken?

Regan. I dare avouch it, sir. What, fifty followers?
Is it not well? What should you need of more?
Yea, or so many, since that both charge and danger
Speak against so great a number? How in one house
Should many people, under two commands,
Hold amity? It's hard; almost impossible.

Goneril. Why might not you, my lord, receive attendance
From those that she calls servants, or from mine?

Regan. Why not, my lord? If then they chanced to slack
you,
We could control them. If you will come to me
(For now I spy a danger), I entreat you
To bring but five-and-twenty. To no more
Will I give place or notice.

Lear. I gave you all—

Regan. And in good time you gave it!

Lear. Made you my guardians, my depositaries;
But kept a reservation to be followed
With such a number. What, must I come to you
With five-and-twenty, Regan? Said you so?

Regan. And speak it again my lord. No more with me.

I looked not for you yet, nor am provided
For your fit welcome.

Lear. Those wicked creatures yet do look well-favored
When others are more wicked; not being the worst
Stands in some rank of praise.
[*To Goneril*] I'll go with you.
Your fifty yet does double five-and-twenty,
And you are twice her love.

Goneril. Hear, me, my lord.
What need you five-and-twenty, ten, or five,
To follow in a house where twice so many
Have a command to tend you?

Regan. What need one?

Lear. O, reason not the need! Our basest beggars
Are in the poorest thing superfluous.
Allow not nature more than nature needs,
Man's life is cheap as beast's. You are a lady:
If only to go warm were gorgeous,
Why, nature needs not what you gorgeous wear
Which scarcely keeps you warm. But, for true need—
You heavens, give me that patience, patience I need!
You see me here, you gods, a poor old man,
As full of grief as age; wretched in both.
If it be you that stirs these daughters' hearts
Against their father, fool me not so much
To bear it tamely; touch me with noble anger,
And let not women's weapons, water drops,
Stain my man's cheeks! No, you unnatural hags!
I will have such revenges on you both
That all the world shall— I will do such things—
What they are yet, I know not; but they shall be
The terrors of the earth! You think I'll weep.
No, I'll not weep.
I have full cause of weeping, but this heart
Shall break into a hundred thousand flaws
Or before I'll weep. O fool, I shall go mad!

[*Exeunt Lear, Gloucester, Kent, and Fool.*]

What need you five-and-twenty, ten, or five,
To follow in a house where twice so many

[*Storm and tempest*]

Cornwall. Let us withdraw; it will be a storm.

Regan. This house is little; the old man and his people
Cannot be well bestowed.

Goneril. It's his own blame; has put himself from rest
And must needs taste his folly.

Regan. For his particular, I'll receive him gladly,
But not one follower.

Goneril. So am I purposed.
Where is my Lord of Gloucester?

Cornwall. Followed the old man forth.

[*Enter Gloucester*]

He is returned.

Gloucester. The King is in high rage.

Cornwall. Where is he going?

Gloucester. He calls to horse, but will I know not where.

Cornwall. It's best to give him way; he leads himself.

Goneril. My lord, entreat him by no means to stay.

Gloucester. Alack, the night comes on, and the bleak
winds
Do sorely ruffle. For many miles about
There's scarce a bush.

Regan. O, sir, to willful men
The injuries that they themselves procure
Must be their schoolmasters. Shut up your doors.
He is attended with a desperate train,
And what they may incense him to, being apt
To have his ear abused, wisdom bids fear.

Cornwall. Shut up your doors, my lord: it is a wild night.
My Regan counsels well. Come out of the storm.

[*Exeunt*]

Act Three

1

[*A heath. Storm still*]

[*Enter Kent and a Gentleman at two doors*]

Kent. Who's there, besides foul weather?

Gentleman. One minded like the weather, most unquietly.

Kent. I know you. Where's the King?

Gentleman. Contending with the fretful elements;
Bids the wind blow the earth into the sea,
Or swell the curled waters above the main,
That things might change or cease; tears his white hair,
Which the impetuous blasts, with eyeless rage,
Catch in their fury and make nothing of;
Strives in his little world of man to outscorn
The to-and-fro-conflicting wind and rain.
This night, wherein the cub-drawn bear would couch,
The lion and the belly-pinched wolf
Keep their fur dry, unbonneted he runs,
And bids what will take all.

Kent. But who is with him?

Gentleman. None but the fool, who labors to outjest
His heart-struck injuries.

But who is with him?

None but the fool, who labors to outjest
His heart-struck injuries.

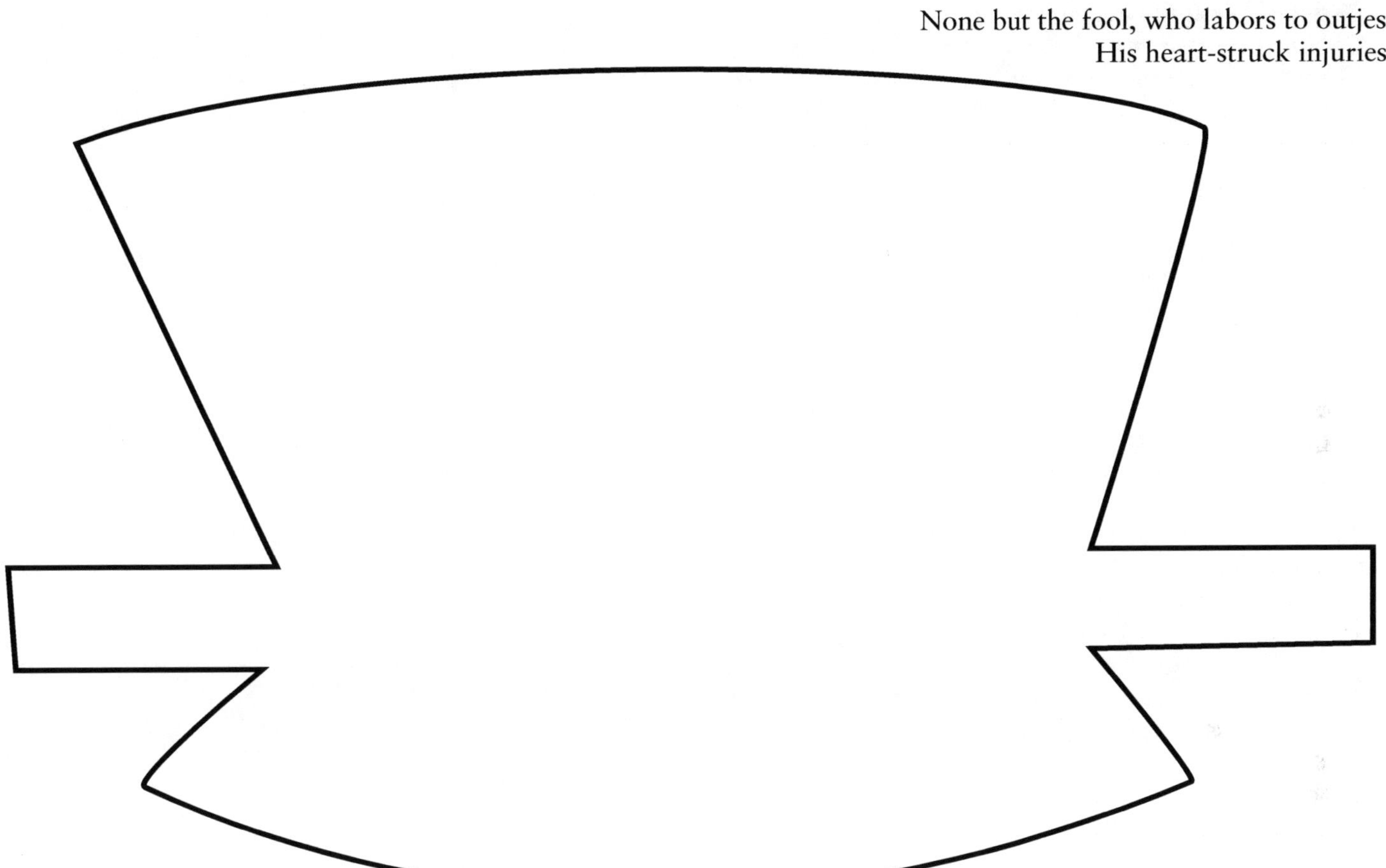

Kent. Sir, I do know you,
And dare upon the warrant of my note
Commend a dear thing to you. There is division
(Although as yet the face of it be covered
With mutual cunning) between Albany and Cornwall;
Who have (as who have not, that their great stars
Throned and set high?) servants, who seem no less,
Which are to France the spies and speculations
Intelligent of our state. What has been seen,
Either in snuffs and packings of the Dukes,
Or the hard rein which both of them have borne
Against the old kind King, or something deeper,
Whereof, perchance, these are but furnishings—
But, true it is, from France there comes a power
Into this scattered kingdom, who already,
Wise in our negligence, have secret feet
In some of our best ports and are at point
To show their open banner. Now to you:
If on my credit you dare build so far
To make your speed to Dover, you shall find
Some that will thank you, making just report
Of how unnatural and bemadding sorrow
The King has cause to plain.
I am a gentleman of blood and breeding,
And from some knowledge and assurance offer
This office to you.

Gentleman. I will talk further with you.

Kent. No, do not.
For confirmation that I am much more
Than my out-wall, open this purse and take
What it contains. If you shall see Cordelia
(As fear not but you shall), show her this ring,
And she will tell you who your fellow is
That yet you do not know. Fie on this storm!
I will go seek the King.

Gentleman. Give me your hand. Have you no more to say?

Kent. Few words, but, to effect, more than all yet:
That, when we have found the King (in which your
pain
That way, I'll this), he that first lights on him
Holla the other.

[*Exeunt severally*]

But, true it is, from France there comes a power
Into this scattered kingdom

2

[Another part of the heath]

[Storm still. Enter Lear and Fool]

Lear. Blow, winds, and crack your cheeks! rage! blow!
You cataracts and hurricanoes, spout
Till you have drenched our steeples, drowned the cocks!
You sulphurous and thought-executing fires,
Vaunt-couriers to oak-cleaving thunderbolts,
Singe my white head! And you, all-shaking thunder,
Strike flat the thick rotundity of the world,
Crack Nature's molds, all germens spill at once,
That makes ingrateful man!

Fool. O nuncle, court holy water in a dry house is better than this rain water out of door. Good nuncle, in, and ask your daughters blessing! Here's a night pities nether wise men nor fools.

Lear. Rumble your bellyful! Spit, fire! spout, rain!
Nor rain, wind, thunder, fire are my daughters.
I tax not you, you elements, with unkindness.
I never gave you kingdom, called you children,
You owe me no subscription. Then let fall
Your horrible pleasure. Here I stand your slave,
A poor, infirm, weak, and despised old man.
But yet I call you servile ministers,
That will with two pernicious daughters join
Your high-engendered battles against a head
So old and white as this! O! O! it is foul!

Fool. He that has a house to put his head in has a good head-piece.
The codpiece that will house
Before the head has any,
The head and he shall louse:
So beggars marry many.
The man that makes his toe
What he his heart should make
Shall of a corn cry woe,
And turn his sleep to wake.
For there was never yet fair woman but she made mouths in a glass.

Rumble your bellyful! Spit, fire! spout, rain!

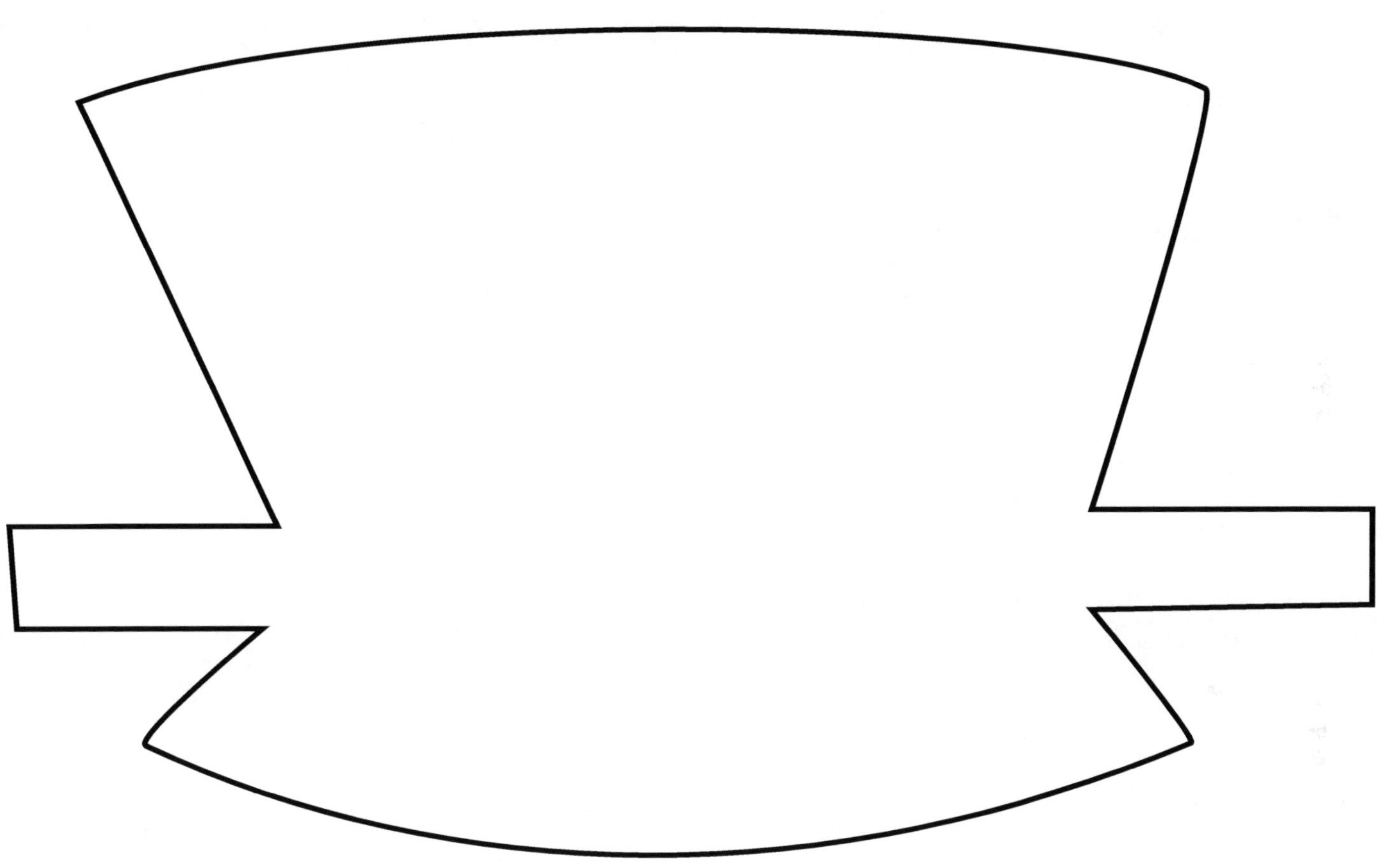

[*Enter Kent*]

Lear. No, I will be the pattern of all patience;
I will say nothing.

Kent. Who's there?

Fool. Marry, here's grace and a codpiece; that's a wise man and a fool.

Kent. Alas, sir, are you here? Things that love night
Love not such nights as these. The wrathful skies
Gallow the very wanderers of the dark
And make them keep their caves. Since I was man,
Such sheets of fire, such bursts of horrid thunder,
Such groans of roaring wind and rain, I never
Remember to have heard. Man's nature cannot carry
The affliction nor the fear.

Lear. Let the great gods,
That keep this dreadful pudder over our heads,
Find out their enemies now. Tremble, you wretch,
That have within you undivulged crimes
Unwhipped of justice. Hide you, you bloody hand;
You perjured, and you simular man of virtue
That are incestuous. Caitiff, in pieces shake
That under covert and convenient seeming
Has practised on man's life. Close pent-up guilts,
Rive your concealing continents, and cry
These dreadful summoners grace. I am a man
More sinned against than sinning.

Kent. Alack, bareheaded?
Gracious my lord, hard by here is a hovel;
Some friendship will it lend you against the tempest.
Repose you there, while I to this hard house
(More harder than the stones whereof it is raised,
Which even but now, demanding after you,
Denied me to come in) return, and force
Their scanted courtesy.

Lear. My wits begin to turn.
Come on, my boy. How do, my boy? Are cold?
I am cold myself. Where is this straw, my fellow?
The art of our necessities is strange,
That can make vile things precious. Come, your hovel.
Poor fool and knave, I have one part in my heart
That's sorry yet for you.

Fool. [*sings*]

He that has and a little tiny wit—
With hey, ho, the wind and the rain—
Must make content with his fortunes fit,
For the rain it rains every day.

Lear. True, my good boy. Come, bring us to this hovel.

[*Exeunt Lear and Kent*]

Tremble, you wretch,
That have within you undivulged crimes
Unwhipped of justice.

Fool. This is a brave night to cool a courtesan.
I'll speak a prophecy before I go:
When priests are more in word than matter;
When brewers mar their malt with water;
When nobles are their tailors' tutors,
No heretics burned, but wenches' suitors;
When every case in law is right,
No squire in debt nor no poor knight;
When slanders do not live in tongues,
Nor cutpurses come not to throngs;
When usurers tell their gold in the field,
And bawds and whores do churches build:
Then shall the realm of Albion
Come to great confusion.
Then comes the time, who lives to see it,
That going shall be used with feet.
This prophecy Merlin shall make, for I live before his
time.

[*Exit Fool*]

I'll speak a prophecy before I go:
When priests are more in word than matter;
When brewers mar their malt with water;

3

[Gloucester's Castle]

[Enter Gloucester and Edmund]

Gloucester. Alack, alack, Edmund, I like not this unnatural dealing! When I desired their leave that I might pity him, they took from me the use of my own house, charged me on pain of perpetual displeasure neither to speak of him, entreat for him, nor any way sustain him.

Edmund. Most savage and unnatural!

Gloucester. Go to; say you nothing. There is division between the Dukes, and a worse matter than that. I have received a letter this night— it is dangerous to be spoken— I have locked the letter in my closet. These injuries the King now bears will be revenged home; there's part of a power already footed; we must incline to the King. I will seek him and privily relieve him. Go you and maintain talk with the Duke, that my charity be not of him perceived. If he ask for me, I am ill and gone to bed. Though I die for it, as no less is threatened me, the King my old master must be relieved. There is some strange thing toward, Edmund. Pray you be careful.

[Exit]

Edmund. This courtesy, forbid you, shall the Duke
Instantly know, and of that letter too.
This seems a fair deserving, and must draw me
That which my father loses— no less than all.
The younger rises when the old does fall.

[Exit]

they took from me the use of my own house, charged me on pain of perpetual displeasure neither to speak of him,

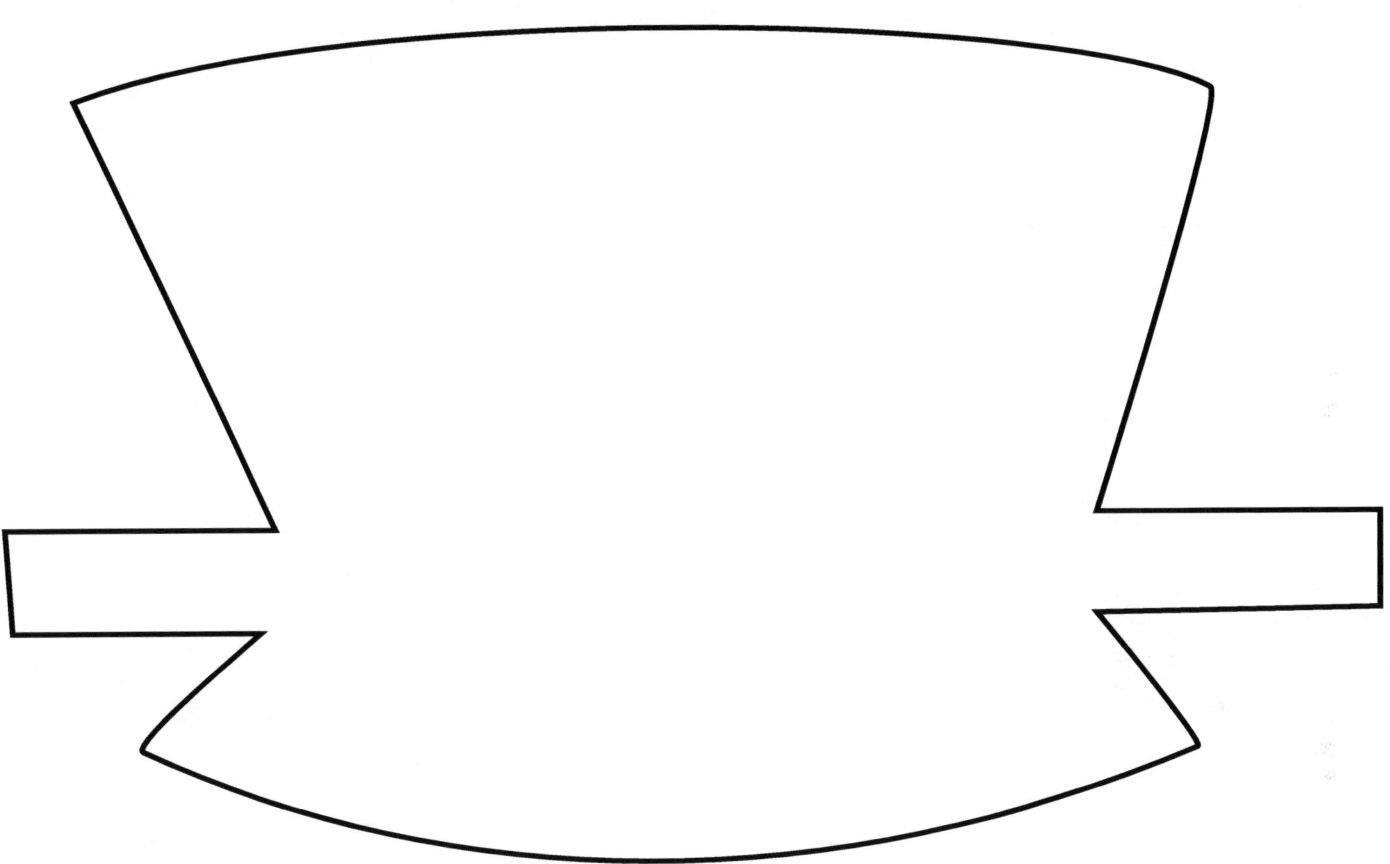

[The heath. Before a hovel]

[Storm still]

[Enter Lear, Kent, and Fool]

Kent. Here is the place, my lord. Good my lord, enter.
The tyranny of the open night is too rough
For nature to endure.

Lear. Let me alone.

Kent. Good my lord, enter here.

Lear. Will break my heart?

Kent. I had rather break my own. Good my lord, enter.

Lear. You think it is much that this contentious storm
Invades us to the skin. So it is to you;
But where the greater malady is fixed,
The lesser is scarce felt. You'd shun a bear;
But if your flight lay toward the raging sea,
You'd meet the bear in the mouth.
When the mind's free,
The body's delicate. The tempest in my mind
Does from my senses take all feeling else
Save what beats there. Filial ingratitude!
Is it not as this mouth should tear this hand
For lifting food to it? But I will punish home!
No, I will weep no more. In such a night
To shut me out! Pour on; I will endure.
In such a night as this! O Regan, Goneril!
Your old kind father, whose frank heart gave all!
O, that way madness lies; let me shun that!
No more of that.

Kent. Good my lord, enter here.

Lear. Please go in yourself; seek your own ease.
This tempest will not give me leave to ponder
On things would hurt me more. But I'll go in.
[To the Fool] In, boy; go first.— You houseless
poverty—
Nay, get you in. I'll pray, and then I'll sleep.

[Exit Fool]

No, I will weep no more. In such a night
To shut me out!

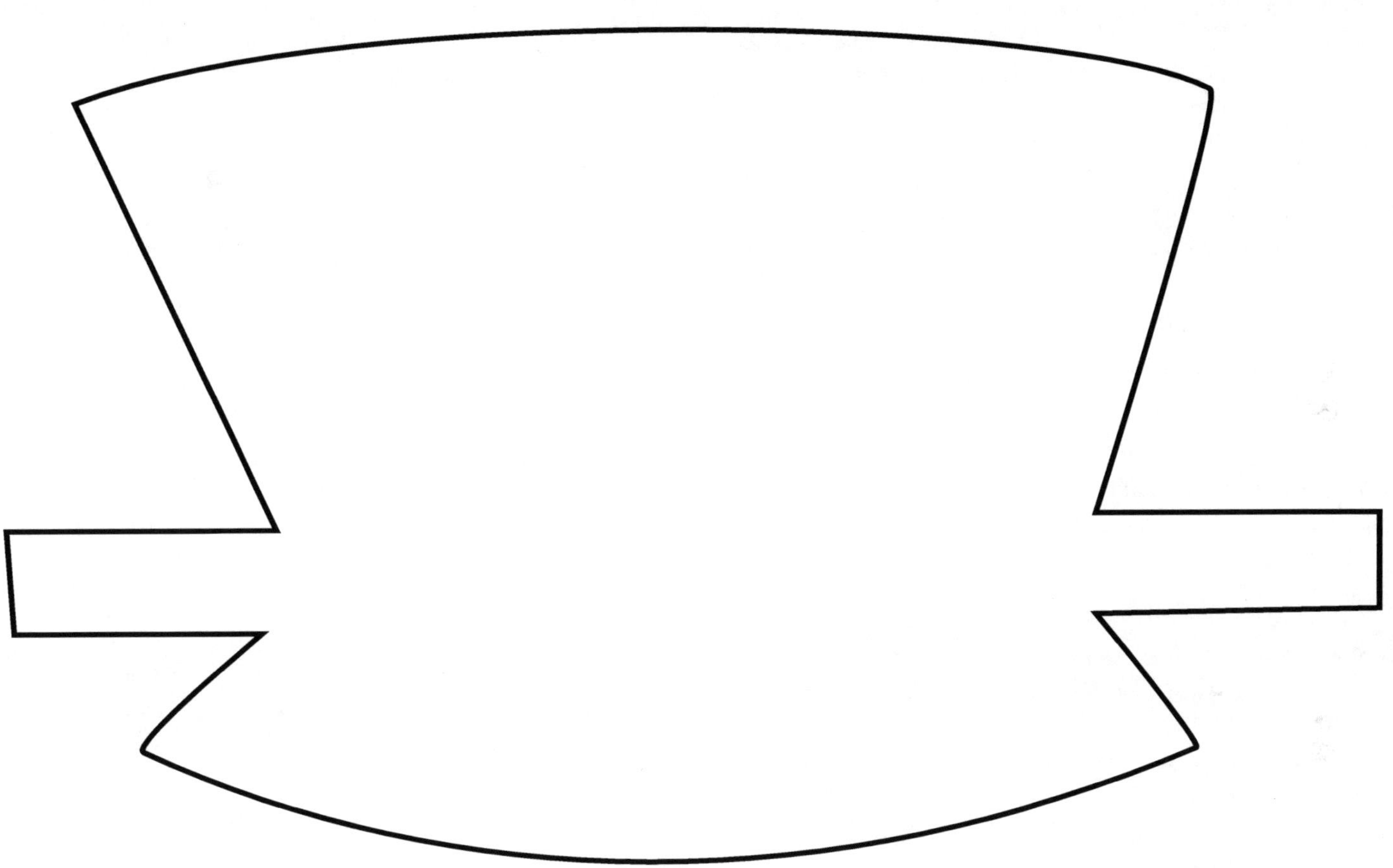

Lear. Poor naked wretches, wheresoe'er you are,
That bide the pelting of this pitiless storm,
How shall your houseless heads and unfed sides,
Your looped and windowed raggedness, defend you
From seasons such as these? O, I have ta'en
Too little care of this! Take physic, pomp;
Expose yourself to feel what wretches feel,
That you may shake the superflux to them
And show the heavens more just.

Edgar. [within] Fathom and half, fathom and half! Poor Tom!

[*Enter Fool from the hovel*]

Fool. Come not in here, nuncle, here's a spirit. Help me, help me!

Kent. Give me your hand. Who's there?

Fool. A spirit, a spirit! He says his name's poor Tom.

Kent. What are you that do grumble there in the straw?
Come forth.

[*Enter Edgar disguised as a madman*]

Edgar. Away! The foul fiend follows me! Through the sharp hawthorn blows the cold wind. Humh! Go to your cold bed, and warm you.

Lear. Have you given all to your two daughters, and are you come to this?

Edgar. Who gives anything to poor Tom? whom the foul fiend has led through fire and through flame, through ford and whirlpool, over bog and quagmire; that has laid knives under his pillow and halters in his pew, set ratsbane by his porridge, made him proud of heart, to ride on a bay trotting horse over four-inched bridges, to course his own shadow for a traitor. Bless your five wits! Tom is acold. O, do de, do de, do de. Bless you from whirlwinds, star-blasting, and taking! Do poor Tom some charity, whom the foul fiend vexes. There could I have him now— and there— and there again— and there!

[*Storm still*]

A spirit, a spirit! He says his name's poor Tom.

Lear. What, have his daughters brought him to this pass?
Could you save nothing? Did you give 'em all?

Fool. Nay, he reserved a blanket, else we had been all shamed.

Lear. Now all the plagues that in the pendulous air
Hang fated over men's faults light on your daughters!

Kent. He has no daughters, sir.

Lear. Death, traitor! Nothing could have subdued nature
To such a lowness but his unkind daughters.
Is it the fashion that discarded fathers
Should have thus little mercy on their flesh?
Judicious punishment! It was this flesh begot
Those pelican daughters.

Edgar. Pillicock sat on Pillicock's Hill. 'Allow, 'allow, loo,
loo!

Fool. This cold night will turn us all to fools and madmen.

Edgar. Take heed of the foul fiend; obey your parents: keep your word justly; swear not; commit not with man's sworn spouse; set not your sweet heart on proud array. Tom's acold.

Lear. What have you been?

Edgar. A servingman, proud in heart and mind; that curled my hair, wore gloves in my cap; served the lust of my mistress' heart and did the act of darkness with her; swore as many oaths as I spoke words, and broke them in the sweet face of heaven; one that slept in the contriving of lust, and waked to do it. Wine loved I deeply, dice dearly; and in woman out-paramoured the Turk. False of heart, light of ear, bloody of hand; hog in sloth, fox in stealth, wolf in greediness, dog in madness, lion in prey. Let not the creaking of shoes nor the rustling of silks betray your poor heart to woman. Keep your foot out of brothel, your hand out of placket, your pen from lender's book, and defy the foul fiend. Still through the hawthorn blows the cold wind; says suum, mun, hey, no, nonny. Dolphin my boy, my boy, sessa! let him trot by.

[*Storm still*]

This cold night will turn us all to fools and madmen.

Lear. Why, you were better in your grave than to answer with your uncovered body this extremity of the skies. Is man no more than this? Consider him well. You owe the worm no silk, the beast no hide, the sheep no wool, the cat no perfume. Ha! Here's three ones are sophisticated! You are the thing itself; unaccommodated man is no more but such a poor, bare, forked animal as you are. Off, off, you lendings! Come, unbutton here.

[*Tears at his clothes.*

Fool. Please, nuncle, be contented! It's a naughty night to swim in. Now a little fire in a wild field were like an old lecher's heart— a small spark, all the rest on his body cold. Look, here comes a walking fire.

[*Enter Gloucester with a torch*]

Edgar. This is the foul fiend Flibbertigibbet. He begins at curfew, and walks till the first cock. He gives the web and the pin, squints the eye, and makes the harelip; mildews the white wheat, and hurts the poor creature of earth.

Saint Withold footed thrice the 'old;
He met the nightmare, and her nine fold;
Bid her alight
And her troth plight,
And aroint you, witch, aroint you!

Kent. How fares your Grace?

Lear. What's he?

Kent. Who's there? What is it you seek?

Gloucester. What are you there? Your names?

Edgar. Poor Tom, that eats the swimming frog, the toad, the tadpole, the wall-newt and the water; that in the fury of his heart, when the foul fiend rages, eats cow-dung for sallets, swallows the old rat and the ditch-dog, drinks the green mantle of the standing pool; who is whipped from tithing to tithing, and stock-punished and imprisoned; who has had three suits to his back, six shirts to his body, horse to ride, and weapons to wear;

But mice and rats, and such small deer, Have been Tom's food for seven long year. Beware my follower. Peace, Smulkin! peace, you fiend!

Gloucester. What, has your Grace no better company?

Edgar. The prince of darkness is a gentleman! Modo he's called, and Mahu.

This is the foul fiend Flibbertigibbet.

Gloucester. Our flesh and blood is grown so vile, my lord,
That it does hate what gets it.

Edgar. Poor Tom's acold.

Gloucester. Go in with me. My duty cannot suffer
To obey in all your daughters' hard commands.
Though their injunction be to bar my doors
And let this tyrannous night take hold upon you,
Yet have I ventured to come seek you out
And bring you where both fire and food is ready.

Lear. First let me talk with this philosopher.
What is the cause of thunder?

Kent. Good my lord, take his offer; go into the house.

Lear. I'll talk a word with this same learned Theban.
What is your study?

Edgar. How to prevent the fiend and to kill vermin.

Lear. Let me ask you one word in private.

Kent. Importune him once more to go, my lord.
His wits begin to unsettle.

Gloucester. Can you blame him?

[*Storm continues*]

His daughters seek his death. Ah, that good Kent!
He said it would be thus— poor banished man!
You say the King grows mad: I'll tell you, friend,
I am almost mad myself. I had a son,
Now outlawed from my blood. He sought my life
But lately, very late. I loved him, friend—
No father his son dearer. True to tell you,
The grief has crazed my wits. What a night is this!
I do beseech your Grace—

Lear. O, cry you mercy, sir.
Noble philosopher, your company.

Edgar. Tom's acold.

Gloucester. In, fellow, there, into the hovel; keep you warm.

Lear. Come, let's in all.

Kent. This way, my lord.

Lear. With him!
I will keep still with my philosopher.

Kent. Good my lord, soothe him; let him take the fellow.

Gloucester. Take him you on.

Kent. Sirrah, come on; go along with us.

Lear. Come, good Athenian.

Gloucester. No words, no words! hush.

Edgar. Child Rowland to the dark tower came;
His word was still

Fie, foh, and fum!
I smell the blood of a British man.

[*Exeunt*]

You say the King grows mad: I'll tell you, friend,
I am almost mad myself

5

[*Gloucester's Castle*]

[*Enter Cornwall and Edmund*]

Cornwall. I will have my revenge before I depart his house.

Edmund. How, my lord, I may be censured, that nature thus gives way to loyalty, something fears me to think of.

Cornwall. I now perceive it was not altogether your brother's evil disposition made him seek his death; but a provoking merit, set awork by a reproveable badness in himself.

Edmund. How malicious is my fortune that I must repent to be just! This is the letter he spoke of, which approves him an intelligent party to the advantages of France. O heavens! that this treason were not—or not I the detector!

Cornwall. Go with me to the Duchess.

Edmund. If the matter of this paper be certain, you have mighty business in hand.

Cornwall. True or false, it has made you Earl of Gloucester.
Seek out where your father is, that he may be ready for our apprehension.

Edmund. [*Aside*] If I find him comforting the King, it will stuff his suspicion more fully.— I will persevere in my course of loyalty, though the conflict be sore between that and my blood.

Cornwall. I will lay trust upon you, and you shall find a dearer father in my love.

[*Exeunt*]

True or false, it has made you Earl of Gloucester.
Seek out where your father is, that he may be ready for our apprehension.

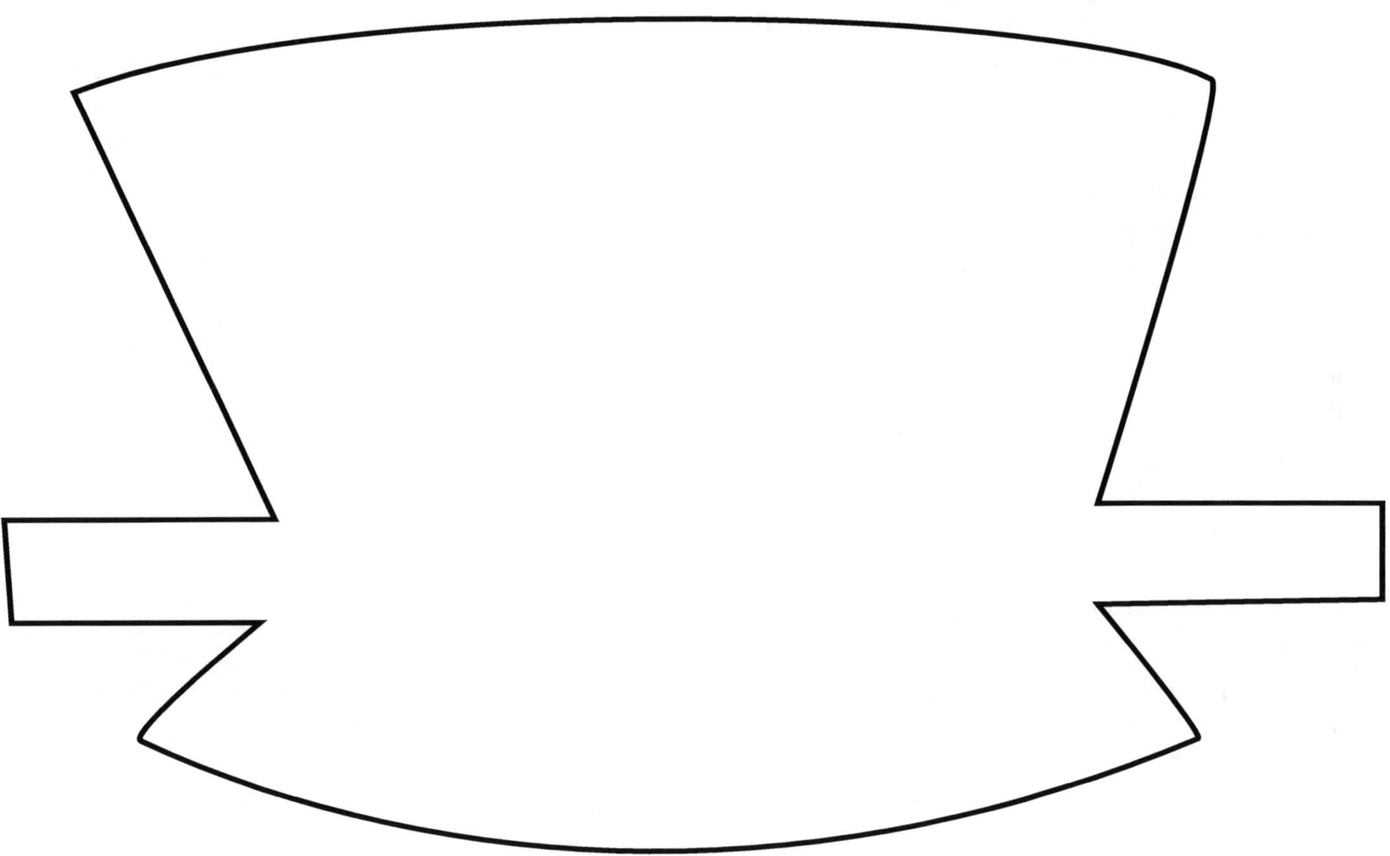

6

[A farmhouse near Gloucester's Castle]

[Enter Gloucester, Lear, Kent, Fool, and Edgar]

Gloucester. Here is better than the open air; take it thankfully. I will piece out the comfort with what addition I can. I will not be long from you.

Kent. All the power of his wits have given way to his
impatience.
The gods reward your kindness!

[Exit Gloucester]

Edgar. Frateretto calls me, and tells me Nero is an angler in the lake of darkness. Pray, innocent, and beware the foul fiend.

Fool. Please, nuncle, tell me whether a madman be a gentleman or a yeoman.

Lear. A king, a king!

Fool. No, he's a yeoman that has a gentleman to his son; for he's a mad yeoman that sees his son a gentleman before him.

Lear. To have a thousand with red burning spits
Come hizzing in upon 'em—

Edgar. The foul fiend bites my back.

Fool. He's mad that trusts in the tameness of a wolf, a horse's health, a boy's love, or a whore's oath.

Lear. It shall be done; I will arraign them straight.
[*To Edgar*] Come, sit you here, most learned justicer.
[*To the Fool*] You, sapient sir, sit here. Now, you she-foxes!

Edgar. Look, where he stands and glares! Want you eyes at trial, madam?
Come over the bourn, Bessy, to me.

Fool. Her boat has a leak,
And she must not speak
Why she dares not come over to you.

he's a mad yeoman that sees his son a gentleman before him.

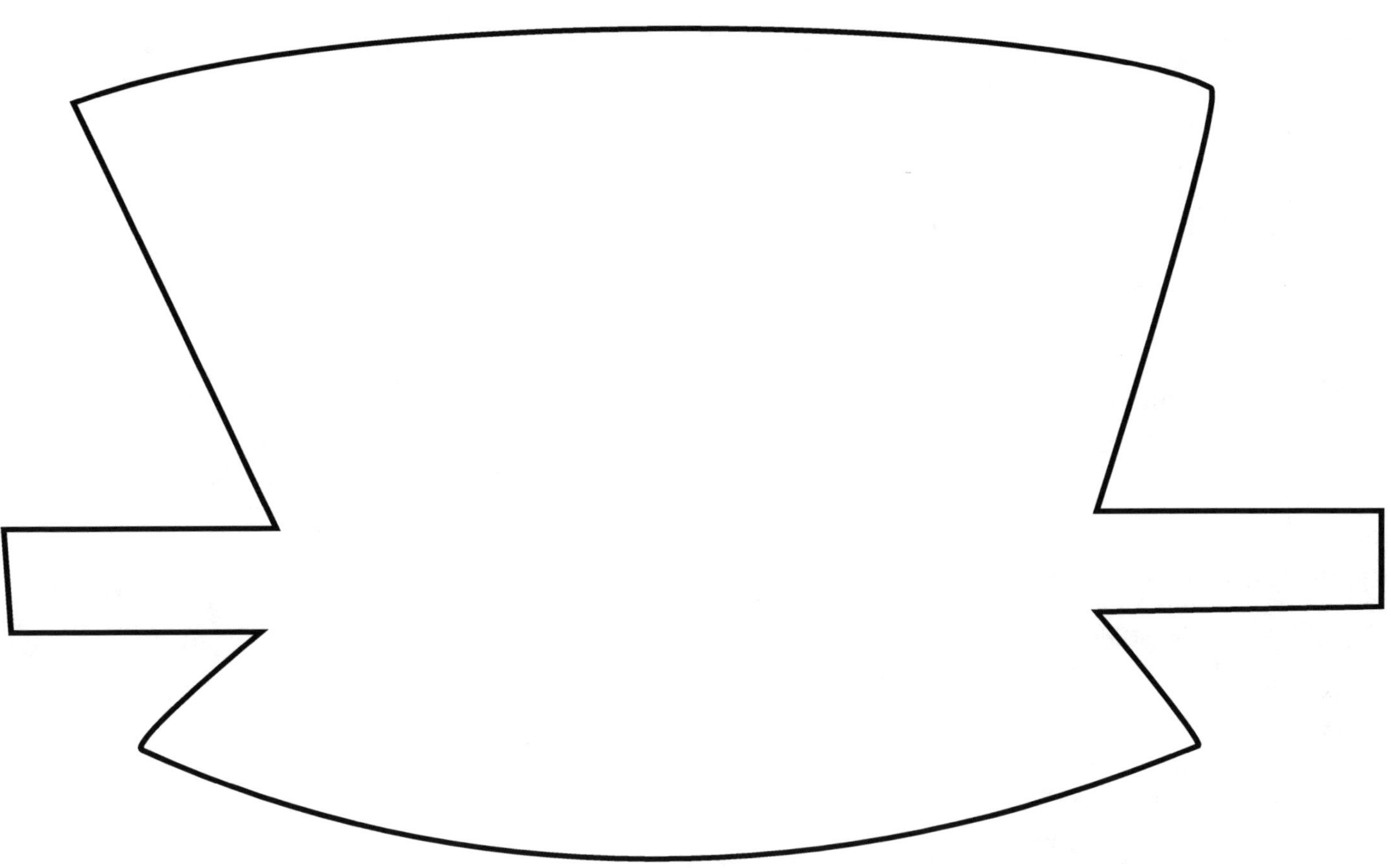

Edgar. The foul fiend haunts poor Tom in the voice of a nightingale. Hoppedance cries in Tom's belly for two white herring. Croak not, black angel; I have no food for you.

Kent. How do you, sir? Stand you not so amazed.
Will you lie down and rest upon the cushions?

Lear. I'll see their trial first. Bring in their evidence.
[*To Edgar*] You, robed man of justice, take your place.
[*To the Fool*] And thou, his yokefellow of equity,
Bench by his side. [*To Kent*] You are of the commission,
Sit you too.

Edgar. Let us deal justly.
Sleep or wake you, jolly shepherd?
Your sheep be in the corn;
And for one blast of your minikin mouth
Your sheep shall take no harm.
Purr! the cat is gray.

Lear. Arraign her first. It's Goneril. I here take my oath before this honorable assembly, she kicked the poor King her father.

Fool. Come here, mistress. Is your name Goneril?

Lear. She cannot deny it.

Fool. Cry you mercy, I took you for a joint-stool.

Lear. And here's another, whose warped looks proclaim
What store her heart is made on. Stop her there!
Arms, arms! sword! fire! Corruption in the place!
False justicer, why have you let her scape?

Edgar. Bless your five wits!

Kent. O pity! Sir, where is the patience now
That you so oft have boasted to retain?

Edgar. [*Aside*] My tears begin to take his part so much
They'll mar my counterfeiting.

Lear. The little dogs and all,
Tray, Blanch, and Sweetheart, see, they bark at me.

Edgar. Tom will throw his head at them. Avaunt, you curs!
Be your mouth or black or white,
Tooth that poisons if it bite;
Mastiff, greyhound, mongrel grim,
Hound or spaniel, brach or lym,
Bobtail tyke or trundle-tall—
Tom will make them weep and wail;
For, with throwing thus my head,

Arms, arms! sword! fire! Corruption in the place!

Dogs leap the hatch, and all are fled.
Do de, de, de. Sessa! Come, march to wakes and fairs and market towns. Poor Tom, your horn is dry.

Lear. Then let them anatomize Regan. See what breeds about her heart. Is there any cause in nature that makes these hard hearts? [*To Edgar*] You, sir— I entertain you for one of my hundred; only I do not like the fashion of your garments. You'll say they are Persian attire; but let them be changed.

Kent. Now, good my lord, lie here and rest awhile.

Lear. Make no noise, make no noise; draw the curtains.
So, so, so. We'll go to supper in the morning. So, so, so.

Fool. And I'll go to bed at noon.

[*Enter Gloucester*]

Gloucester. Come here, friend. Where is the King my master?

Kent. Here, sir; but trouble him not; his wits are gone.

Gloucester. Good friend, please take him in your arms.
I have overheard a plot of death upon him.
There is a litter ready; lay him in it
And drive towards Dover, friend, where you shall meet
Both welcome and protection. Take up your master.
If you should dally half an hour, his life,
With yours, and all that offer to defend him,
Stand in assured loss. Take up, take up!
And follow me, that will to some provision
Give you quick conduct.

Kent. Oppressed nature sleeps.
This rest might yet have balmed your broken senses,
Which, if convenience will not allow,
Stand in hard cure. [*To the Fool*] Come, help to bear your master.
You must not stay behind.

Gloucester. Come, come, away!

[*Exeunt all but Edgar*]

Edgar. When we our betters see bearing our woes,
We scarcely think our miseries our foes.
Who alone suffers suffers most in the mind,
Leaving free things and happy shows behind;
But then the mind much sufferance does overskip
When grief has mates, and bearing fellowship.
How light and portable my pain seems now,
When that which makes me bend makes the King bow,
He childed as I fathered! Tom, away!

Good friend, please take him in your arms.
I have overheard a plot of death upon him.

Mark the high noises, and yourself bewray
When false opinion, whose wrong thought defiles
 you,
In your just proof repeals and reconciles you.
What will hap more tonight, safe scape the King!
Lurk, lurk.

[*Exit*]

[Gloucester's Castle]

[Enter Cornwall, Regan, Goneril, Edmund the Bastard, and Servants]

Cornwall. [*To Goneril*] Post speedily to my lord your husband, show him this letter. The army of France is landed.— Seek out the traitor Gloucester.

[Exeunt some of the Servants]

Regan. Hang him instantly.

Goneril. Pluck out his eyes.

Cornwall. Leave him to my displeasure. Edmund, keep you our sister company. The revenges we are bound to take upon your traitorous father are not fit for your beholding. Advise the Duke where you are going, to a most festinate preparation. We are bound to the like. Our posts shall be swift and intelligent between us. Farewell, dear sister; farewell, my Lord of Gloucester.

[Enter Oswald the Steward]

How now? Where's the King?

Oswald. My Lord of Gloucester has conveyed him hence.
Some five or six and thirty of his knights,
Hot questrists after him, met him at gate;
Who, with some other of the lord's dependants,
Are gone with him towards Dover, where they boast
To have well-armed friends.

Cornwall. Get horses for your mistress.

Goneril. Farewell, sweet lord, and sister.

Cornwall. Edmund, farewell.

[Exeunt Goneril, Edmund, and Oswald]

Go seek the traitor Gloucester,
Pinion him like a thief, bring him before us.

[Exeunt other Servants]

The revenges we are bound to take upon your traitorous father are not fit for your beholding.

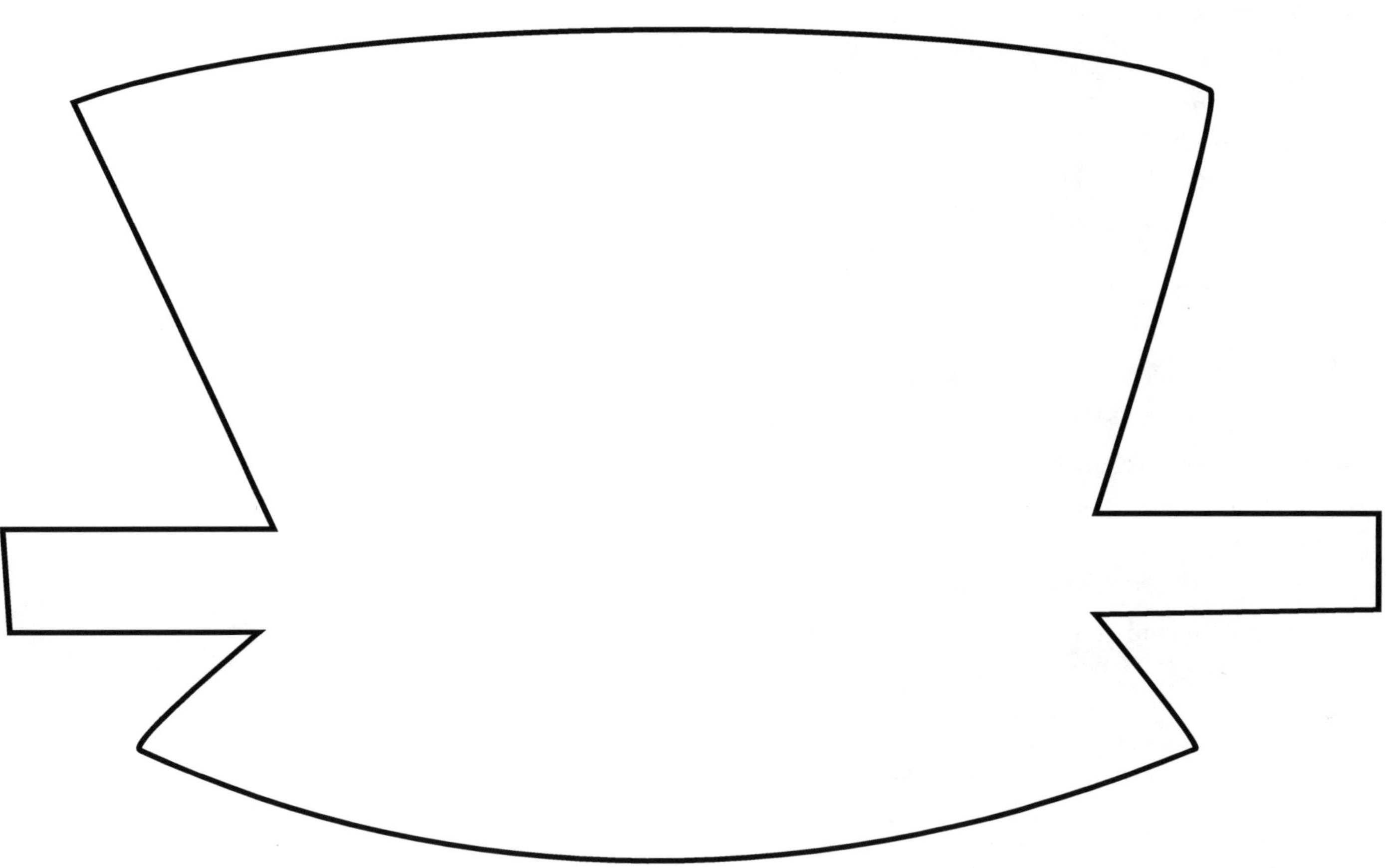

Cornwall. Though well we may not pass upon his life
Without the form of justice, yet our power
Shall do a courtesy to our wrath, which men
May blame, but not control.

[*Enter Gloucester, brought in by two or three.*

Who's there? the traitor?

Regan. Ingrateful fox! it is he.

Cornwall. Bind fast his corky arms.

Gloucester. What mean your Graces? Good my friends, consider
You are my guests. Do me no foul play, friends.

Cornwall. Bind him, I say.

[*Servants bind him*]

Regan. Hard, hard. O filthy traitor!

Gloucester. Unmerciful lady as you are, I am none.

Cornwall. To this chair bind him. Villain, you shall find—

[*Regan plucks his beard*]

Gloucester. By the kind gods, it is most ignobly done
To pluck me by the beard.

Regan. So white, and such a traitor!

Gloucester. Naughty lady,
These hairs which you do ravish from my chin
Will quicken, and accuse you. I am your host.
With robber's hands my hospitable favors
You should not ruffle thus. What will you do?

Cornwall. Come, sir, what letters had you late from France?

Regan. Be simple-answered, for we know the truth.

Cornwall. And what confederacy have you with the traitors
Late footed in the kingdom?

Regan. To whose hands have you sent the lunatic King?
Speak.

Gloucester. I have a letter guessingly set down,
Which came from one that's of a neutral heart,
And not from one opposed.

Cornwall. Cunning.

Regan. And false.

Naughty lady,
These hairs which you do ravish from my chin
Will quicken, and accuse you.

Cornwall. Where have you sent the King?

Gloucester. To Dover.

Regan. Wherefore to Dover? Were you not charged at peril—

Cornwall. Wherefore to Dover? Let him first answer that.

Gloucester. I am tied to the stake, and I must stand the course.

Regan. Wherefore to Dover, sir?

Gloucester. Because I would not see your cruel nails
Pluck out his poor old eyes; nor your fierce sister
In his anointed flesh stick boarish fangs.
The sea, with such a storm as his bare head
In hell-black night endured, would have buoyed up
And quenched the steeled fires.
Yet, poor old heart, he helped the heavens to rain.
If wolves had at your gate howled that stern time,
You should have said, "Good porter, turn the key."
All cruels else subscribed. But I shall see
The winged vengeance overtake such children.

Cornwall. See it shall you never. Fellows, hold the chair.
Upon these eyes of yours I'll set my foot.

Gloucester. He that will think to live till he be old,
Give me some help!— O cruel! O you gods!

Regan. One side will mock another. The other too!

Cornwall. If you see vengeance—

First Servant. Hold your hand, my lord!
I have served you ever since I was a child;
But better service have I never done you
Than now to bid you hold.

Regan. How now, you dog?

First Servant. If you did wear a beard upon your chin,
I'd shake it on this quarrel.

Regan. What do you mean?

Cornwall. My villain! Draw and fight.

First Servant. Nay, then, come on, and take the chance of anger.

Regan. Give me your sword. A peasant stand up thus?

[*She takes a sword and runs at him behind*]

First Servant. O, I am slain! My lord, you have one eye left
To see some mischief on him. O!

[*He dies*]

See it shall you never. Fellows, hold the chair.
Upon these eyes of yours I'll set my foot.

Cornwall. Lest it see more, prevent it. Out, vile jelly!
Where is your lustre now?

Gloucester. All dark and comfortless! Where's my son
Edmund?
Edmund, enkindle all the sparks of nature
To quit this horrid act.

Regan. Out, treacherous villain!
You call on him that hates you. It was he
That made the overture of your treasons to us;
Who is too good to pity you.

Gloucester. O my follies! Then Edgar was abused.
Kind gods, forgive me that, and prosper him!

Regan. Go thrust him out at gates, and let him smell
His way to Dover.

[*Exit one with Gloucester*]

How is it, my lord? How look you?

Cornwall. I have received a hurt. Follow me, lady.
Turn out that eyeless villain. Throw this slave
Upon the dunghill. Regan, I bleed apace.
Untimely comes this hurt. Give me your arm.

[*Exit Cornwall, led by Regan*]

Second Servant. I'll never care what wickedness I do,
If this man come to good.

Third Servant. If she live long,
And in the end meet the old course of death,
Women will all turn monsters.

Second Servant. Let's follow the old Earl, and get the
bedlam
To lead him where he would. His roguish madness
Allows itself to anything.

Third Servant. Go you. I'll fetch some flax and whites of
eggs
To apply to his bleeding face. Now heaven help him!

[*Exeunt*]

O my follies! Then Edgar was abused.
Kind gods, forgive me that, and prosper him!

Act Four

1

[The heath]

[Enter Edgar]

Edgar. Yet better thus, and known to be contemned,
Than still contemned and flattered. To be worst,
The lowest and most dejected thing of fortune,
Stands still in esperance, lives not in fear.
The lamentable change is from the best;
The worst returns to laughter. Welcome then,
You unsubstantial air that I embrace!
The wretch that you have blown unto the worst
Owes nothing to your blasts.

[Enter Gloucester, led by an Old Man]

But who comes here?
My father, poorly led? World, world, O world!
But that your strange mutations make us hate you,
Life would not yield to age.

Old Man. O my good lord,
I have been your tenant, and your father's tenant,
These fourscore years.

Gloucester. Away, get you away! Good friend, be gone.
Your comforts can do me no good at all;
You they may hurt.

Old Man. You cannot see your way.

Gloucester. I have no way, and therefore want no eyes;
I stumbled when I saw. Full oft it is seen
Our means secure us, and our mere defects
Prove our commodities. Ah dear son Edgar,
The food of your abused father's wrath!
Might I but live to see you in my touch,
I'd say I had eyes again!

Old Man. How now? Who's there?

The worst returns to laughter. Welcome then,
You unsubstantial air that I embrace!

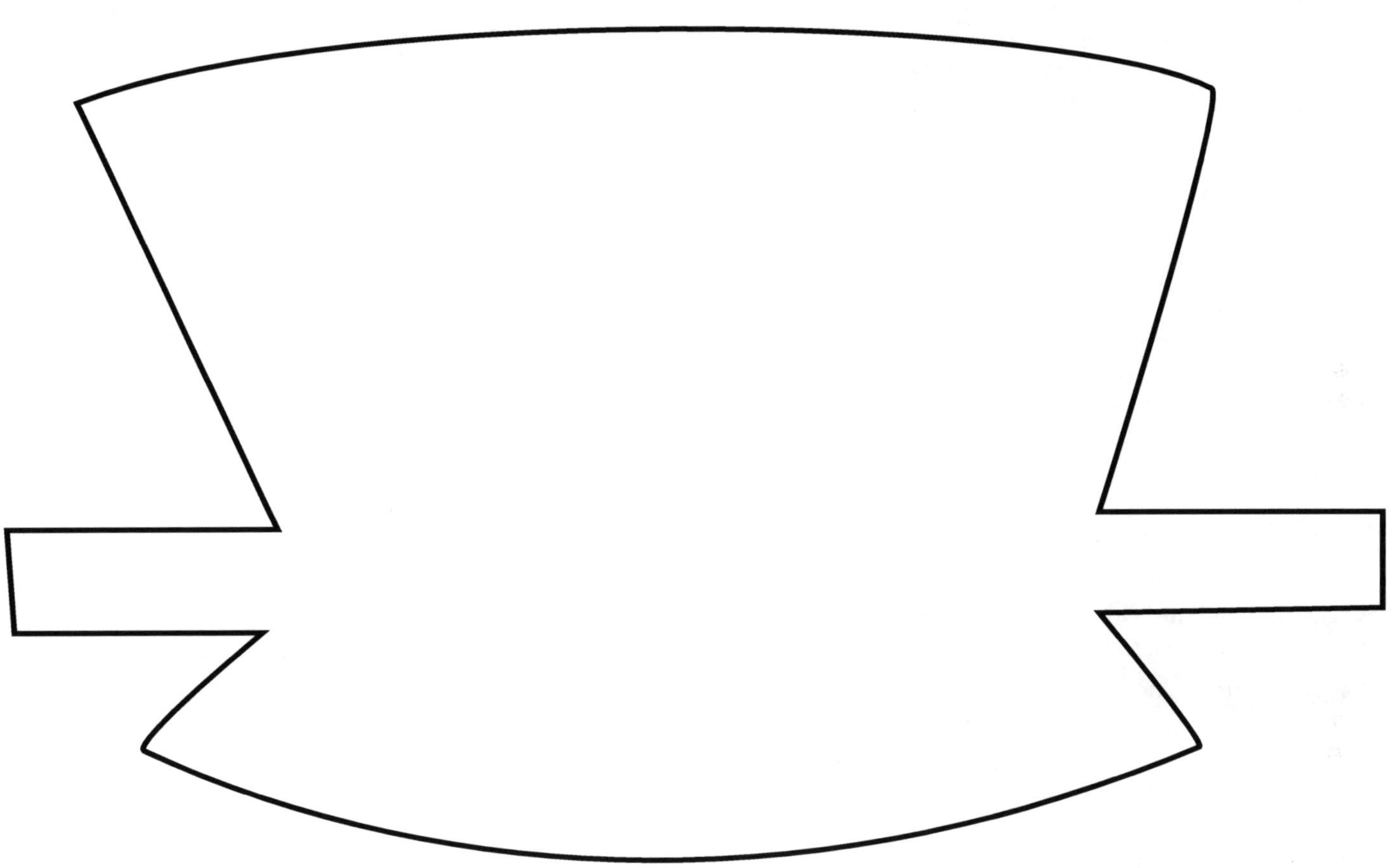

Edgar. [*Aside*] O gods! Who is it can say "I am at the worst"?
I am worse than ever I was.

Old Man. It's poor mad Tom.

Edgar. [*Aside*] And worse I may be yet. The worst is not
So long as we can say "This is the worst."

Old Man. Fellow, where goest?

Gloucester. Is it a beggarman?

Old Man. Madman and beggar too.

Gloucester. He has some reason, else he could not beg.
In the last night's storm I such a fellow saw,
Which made me think a man a worm. My son
Came then into my mind, and yet my mind
Was then scarce friends with him. I have heard more since.
As flies to wanton boys are we to the gods.
They kill us for their sport.

Edgar. [*Aside*] How should this be?
Bad is the trade that must play fool to sorrow,
Angering itself and others.— Bless you, master!

Gloucester. Is that the naked fellow?

Old Man. Ay, my lord.

Gloucester. Then please get you gone. If for my sake
You will overtake us hence a mile or twain
In the way toward Dover, do it for ancient love;
And bring some covering for this naked soul,
Who I'll entreat to lead me.

Old Man. Alack, sir, he is mad!

Gloucester. It's the time's plague when madmen lead the blind.
Do as I bid you, or rather do your pleasure.
Above the rest, be gone.

Old Man. I'll bring him the best apparel that I have,
Come on it what will.

[*Exit Old Man*]

In the last night's storm I such a fellow saw,
Which made me think a man a worm.

Gloucester. Sirrah naked fellow—

Edgar. Poor Tom's acold. [*Aside*] I cannot daub it further.

Gloucester. Come here, fellow.

Edgar. [*Aside*] And yet I must.— Bless your sweet eyes,
they bleed.

Gloucester. Know you the way to Dover?

Edgar. Both stile and gate, horseway and footpath.
Poor Tom has been scared out of his good wits.
Bless you, good man's son, from the foul fiend!
Five fiends have been in poor Tom at once:
of lust, as Obidicut; Hobbididence, prince of
dumbness; Mahu, of stealing; Modo, of murder;
Flibbertigibbet, of mopping and mowing, who
since possesses chambermaids and waiting women.
So, bless you, master!

Gloucester. Here, take this purse, you whom the heavens'
plagues
Have humbled to all strokes. That I am wretched
Makes you the happier. Heavens, deal so still!
Let the superfluous and lust-dieted man,
That slaves your ordinance, that will not see
Because he does not feel, feel your power quickly;
So distribution should undo excess,
And each man have enough. Do you know Dover?

Edgar. Ay, master.

Gloucester. There is a cliff, whose high and bending head
Looks fearfully in the confined deep.
Bring me but to the very brim of it,
And I'll repair the misery you do bear
With something rich about me. From that place
I shall no leading need.

Edgar. Give me your arm.
Poor Tom shall lead you.

[*Exeunt*]

There is a cliff, whose high and bending head
Looks fearfully in the confined deep.
Bring me but to the very brim of

2

[Before the Duke of Albany's Palace]

[Enter Goneril and Edmund the Bastard]

Goneril. Welcome, my lord. I marvel our mild husband
Not met us on the way.

[Enter Oswald the Steward.

Now, where's your master?

Oswald. Madam, within, but never man so changed.
I told him of the army that was landed:
He smiled at it. I told him you were coming:
His answer was, "The worse." Of Gloucester's treachery
And of the loyal service of his son
When I informed him, then he called me sot
And told me I had turned the wrong side out.
What most he should dislike seems pleasant to him;
What like, offensive.

Goneril. [*To Edmund*] Then shall you go no further.
It is the cowish terror of his spirit,
That dares not undertake. He'll not feel wrongs
Which tie him to an answer. Our wishes on the way
May prove effects. Back, Edmund, to my brother.
Hasten his musters and conduct his powers.
I must change arms at home and give the distaff
Into my husband's hands. This trusty servant
Shall pass between us. Before long you are like to hear
(If you dare venture in your own behalf)
A mistress's command. Wear this.

[Gives a favor]

Spare speech.
Decline your head. This kiss, if it dare speak,
Would stretch your spirits up into the air.
Conceive, and fare you well.

Edmund. Yours in the ranks of death!

[Exit Edmund]

Goneril. My most dear Gloucester!
O, the difference of man and man!
To you a woman's services are due;
My fool usurps my body.

Oswald. Madam, here comes my lord.

[Exit Oswald]

I told him you were coming:
His answer was, "The worse."

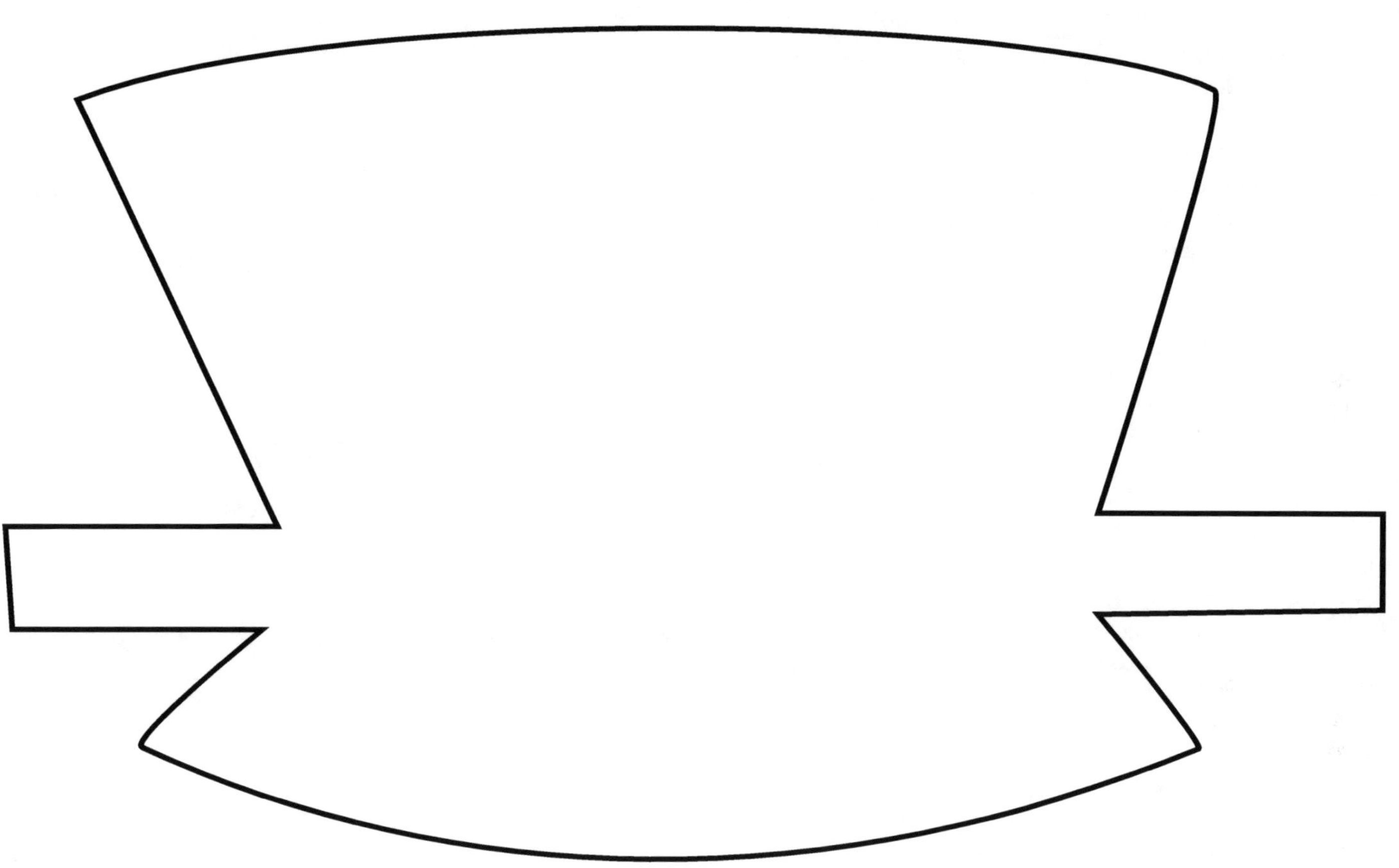

[*Enter Albany*]

Goneril. I have been worth the whistle.

Albany. O Goneril,
You are not worth the dust which the rude wind
Blows in your face! I fear your disposition.
That nature which contemns it origin
Cannot be bordered certain in itself.
She that herself will sliver and disbranch
From her material sap, perforce must wither
And come to deadly use.

Goneril. No more! The text is foolish.

Albany. Wisdom and goodness to the vile seem vile;
Filths savor but themselves. What have you done?
Tigers, not daughters, what have you performed?
A father, and a gracious aged man,
Whose reverence even the head-lugged bear would
lick,
Most barbarous, most degenerate, have you madded.
Could my good brother suffer you to do it?
A man, a prince, by him so benefited!
If that the heavens do not their visible spirits
Send quickly down to tame these vile offences,
It will come,
Humanity must perforce prey on itself,
Like monsters of the deep.

Goneril. Milk-livered man!
That bear a cheek for blows, a head for wrongs;
Who have not in your brows an eye discerning
Your honor from your suffering; that not know
Fools do those villains pity who are punished
Before they have done their mischief. Where's your
drum?
France spreads his banners in our noiseless land,
With plumed helm your state begins to threat,
While you, a moral fool, sit still, and cry
"Alack, why does he so?"

Albany. See yourself, devil!
Proper deformity seems not in the fiend
So horrid as in woman.

Goneril. O vain fool!

Albany. You changed and self-covered thing, for shame!
Bemonster not your feature! Were it my fitness
To let these hands obey my blood,
They are apt enough to dislocate and tear
Your flesh and bones. However you are a fiend,
A woman's shape does shield you.

Goneril. Marry, your manhood mew!

France spreads his banners in our noiseless land,
With plumed helm your state begins to threat,
While you, a moral fool, sit still, and cry
"Alack, why does he so?"

[*Enter a Gentleman*]

Albany. What news?

Gentleman. O, my good lord, the Duke of Cornwall's dead,
Slain by his servant, going to put out
The other eye of Gloucester.

Albany. Gloucester's eyes?

Gentleman. A servant that he bred, thrilled with remorse,
Opposed against the act, bending his sword
To his great master; who, thereat enraged,
Flew on him, and among them felled him dead;
But not without that harmful stroke which since
Have plucked him after.

Albany. This shows you are above,
You justicers, that these our nether crimes
So speedily can venge! But O poor Gloucester!
Lose he his other eye?

Gentleman. Both, both, my lord.
This letter, madam, craves a speedy answer.
It's from your sister.

Goneril. [*Aside*] One way I like this well;
But being widow, and my Gloucester with her,
May all the building in my fancy pluck
Upon my hateful life. Another way
The news is not so tart.— I'll read, and answer.

[*Exit Goneril*]

Albany. Where was his son when they did take his eyes?

Gentleman. Come with my lady here.

Albany. He is not here.

Gentleman. No, my good lord; I met him back again.

Albany. Knows he the wickedness?

Gentleman. Ay, my good lord. It was he informed against him,
And quit the house on purpose, that their punishment
Might have the freer course.

Albany. Gloucester, I live
To thank you for the love you showed the King,
And to revenge your eyes. Come here, friend.
Tell me what more you know.

[*Exeunt*]

O, my good lord, the Duke of Cornwall's dead,
Slain by his servant, going to put out
The other eye of Gloucester.

[The French camp near Dover]

[Enter Kent and a Gentleman]

Kent. Why the King of France is so suddenly gone back know you the reason?

Gentleman. Something he left imperfect in the state, which since his coming forth is thought of, which imports to the kingdom so much fear and danger that his personal return was most required and necessary.

Kent. Who has he left behind him general?

Gentleman. The Marshal of France, Monsieur La Far.

Kent. Did your letters pierce the Queen to any demonstration of grief?

Gentleman. Ay, sir. She took them, read them in my presence,
And now and then an ample tear trilled down
Her delicate cheek. It seemed she was a queen
Over her passion, who, most rebel-like,
Sought to be king over her.

Kent. O, then it moved her?

Gentleman. Not to a rage. Patience and sorrow strove
Who should express her goodliest. You have seen
Sunshine and rain at once: her smiles and tears
Were like, a better way. Those happy smilets
That played on her ripe lip seemed not to know
What guests were in her eyes, which parted thence
As pearls from diamonds dropped. In brief,
Sorrow would be a rarity most beloved,
If all could so become it.

Kent. Made she no verbal question?

And now and then an ample tear trilled down
Her delicate cheek.

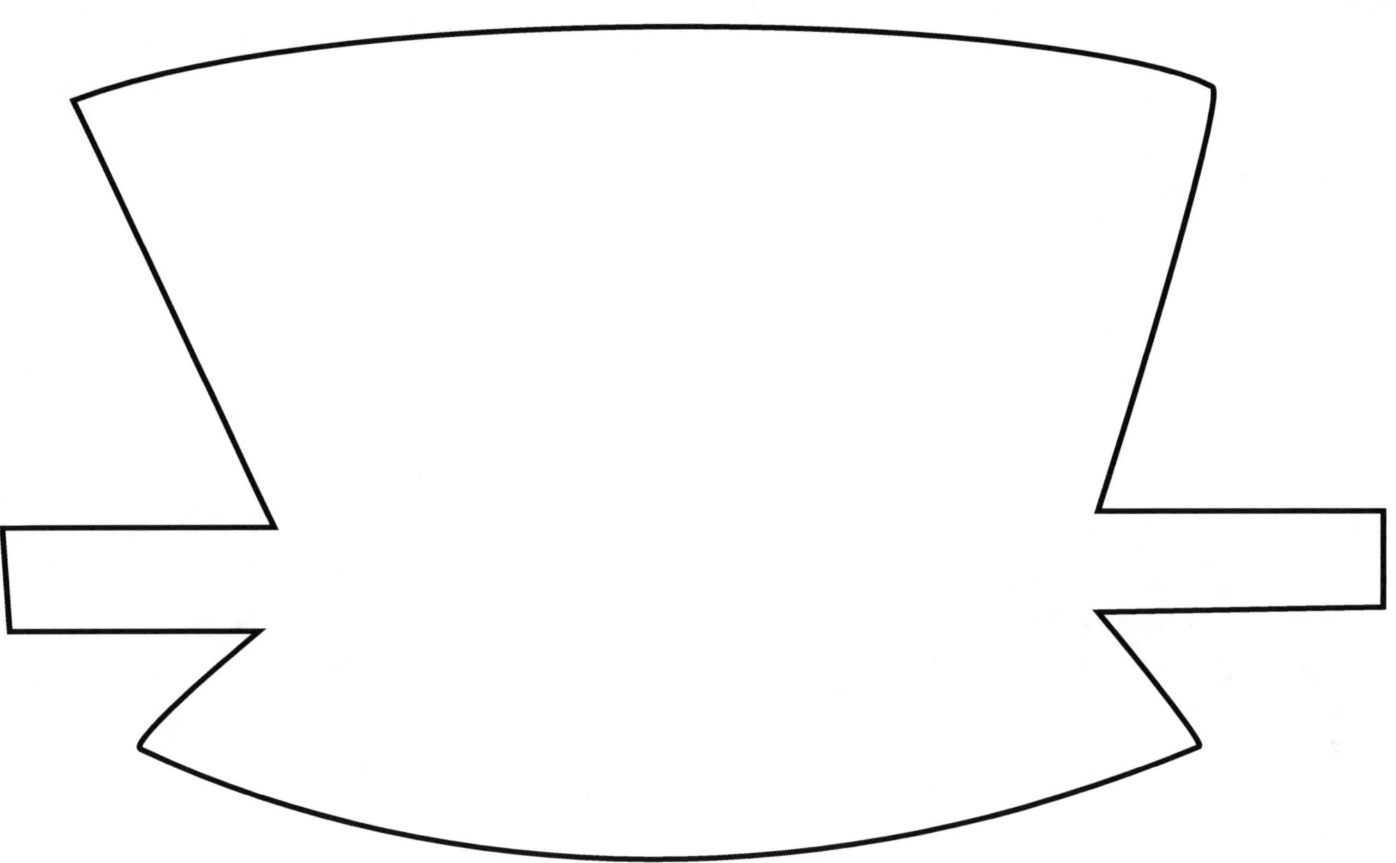

Gentleman. Faith, once or twice she heaved the name of father
Pantingly forth, as if it pressed her heart;
Cried "Sisters, sisters! Shame of ladies! Sisters!
Kent! father! sisters! What, in the storm? in the night?
Let pity not be believed!" There she shook
The holy water from her heavenly eyes,
And clamor moistened. Then away she started
To deal with grief alone.

Kent. It is the stars,
The stars above us, govern our conditions;
Else one self mate and mate could not beget
Such different issues. You spoke not with her since?

Gentleman. No.

Kent. Was this before the King returned?

Gentleman. No, since.

Kent. Well, sir, the poor distressed Lear's in the town;
Who sometime, in his better tune, remembers
What we are come about, and by no means
Will yield to see his daughter.

Gentleman. Why, good sir?

Kent. A sovereign shame so elbows him; his own unkindness,
That stripped her from his benediction, turned her
To foreign casualties, gave her dear rights
To his dog-hearted daughters— these things sting
His mind so venomously that burning shame
Detains him from Cordelia.

Gentleman. Alack, poor gentleman!

Kent. Of Albany's and Cornwall's powers you heard not?

Gentleman. It's so; they are afoot.

Kent. Well, sir, I'll bring you to our master Lear
And leave you to attend him. Some dear cause
Will in concealment wrap me up awhile.
When I am known aright, you shall not grieve
Lending me this acquaintance. I pray you go
Along with me.

[*Exeunt*]

Well, sir, the poor distressed Lear's in the town;
Who sometime, in his better tune, remembers
What we are come about

[The French camp]

[Enter, with Drum and Colors, Cordelia, Doctor, and Soldiers]

Cordelia. Alack, it is he! Why, he was met even now
As mad as the vexed sea, singing aloud,
Crowned with rank fumiter and furrow weeds,
With hardocks, hemlock, nettles, cuckoo flowers,
Darnel, and all the idle weeds that grow
In our sustaining Cornwall. A century send forth.
Search every acre in the high-grown field
And bring him to our eye.

[Exit an Officer]

What can man's wisdom
In the restoring his bereaved sense?
He that helps him take all my outward worth.

Doctor. There is means, madam.
Our foster nurse of nature is repose,
The which he lacks. That to provoke in him
Are many simples operative, whose power
Will close the eye of anguish.

Cordelia. All blessed secrets,
All you unpublished virtues of the earth,
Spring with my tears! be aidant and remediate
In the good man's distress! Seek, seek for him!
Lest his ungoverned rage dissolve the life
That wants the means to lead it.

[Enter Messenger]

Messenger. News, madam.
The British powers are marching hereward.

Cordelia. It's known before. Our preparation stands
In expectation of them. O dear father,
It is your business that I go about.
Therefore great France
My mourning and important tears has pitied.
No blown ambition does our arms incite,
But love, dear love, and our aged father's right.
Soon may I hear and see him!

[Exeunt]

What can man's wisdom
In the restoring his bereaved sense?

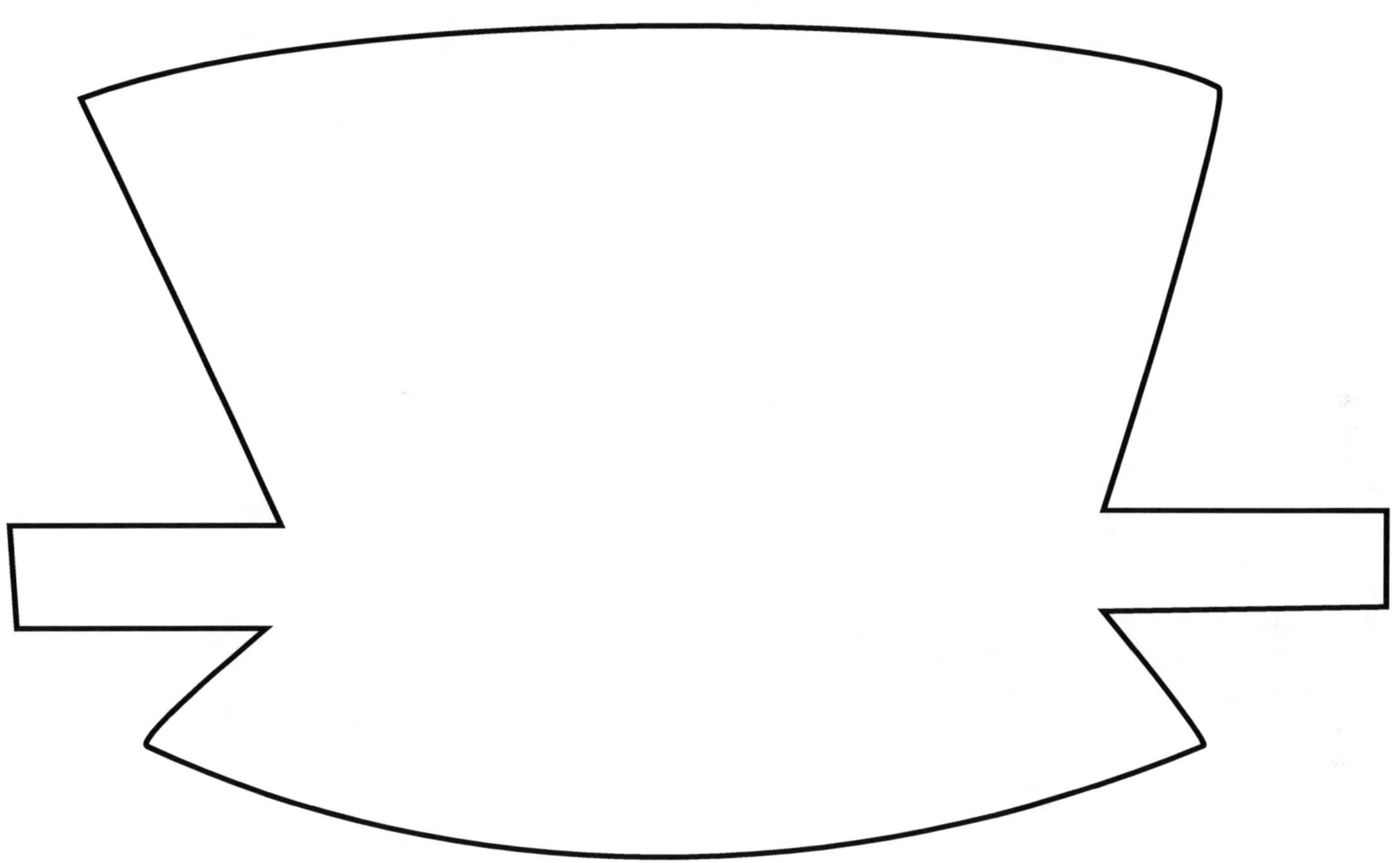

5

[*Gloucester's Castle*]

[*Enter Regan and Oswald the Steward*]

Regan. But are my brother's powers set forth?

Oswald. Ay, madam.

Regan. Himself in person there?

Oswald. Madam, with much ado.
Your sister is the better soldier.

Regan. Lord Edmund spoke not with your lord at home?

Oswald. No, madam.

Regan. What might import my sister's letter to him?

Oswald. I know not, lady.

Regan. Faith, he is posted hence on serious matter.
It was great ignorance, Gloucester's eyes being out,
To let him live. Where he arrives he moves
All hearts against us. Edmund, I think, is gone,
In pity of his misery, to dispatch
His nighted life; moreover, to descry
The strength of the enemy.

Oswald. I must needs after him, madam, with my letter.

Regan. Our troops set forth tomorrow. Stay with us.
The ways are dangerous.

Oswald. I may not, madam.
My lady charged my duty in this business.

Regan. Why should she write to Edmund? Might not you
Transport her purposes by word? Belike,
Something— I know not what— I'll love you much—
Let me unseal the letter.

It was great ignorance, Gloucester's eyes being out,
To let him live.

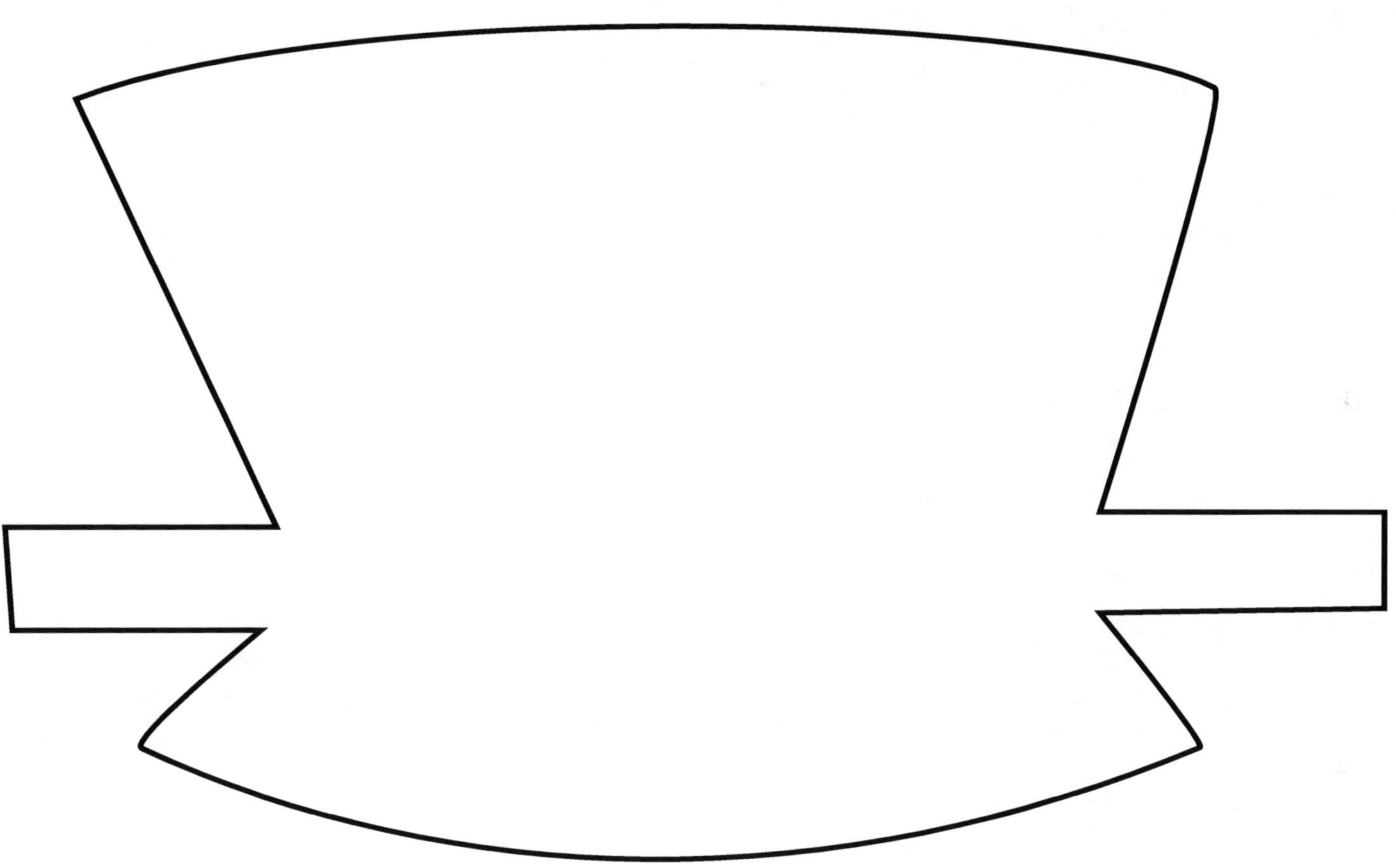

Oswald. Madam, I had rather—

Regan. I know your lady does not love her husband;
I am sure of that; and at her late being here
She gave strange oeillades and most speaking looks
To noble Edmund. I know you are of her bosom.

Oswald. I, madam?

Regan. I speak in understanding. You are! I know it.
Therefore I do advise you take this note.
My lord is dead; Edmund and I have talked,
And more convenient is he for my hand
Than for your lady's. You may gather more.
If you do find him, pray you give him this;
And when your mistress hears thus much from you,
I pray desire her call her wisdom to her.
So farewell.
If you do chance to hear of that blind traitor,
Preferment falls on him that cuts him off.

Oswald. Would I could meet him, madam! I should show
What party I do follow.

Regan. Fare you well.

[*Exeunt*]

She gave strange oeillades and most speaking looks
To noble Edmund. I know you are of her bosom.

[*The country near Dover*]

[*Enter Gloucester, and Edgar like a peasant*]

Gloucester. When shall I come to the top of that same hill?

Edgar. You do climb up it now. Look how we labor.

Gloucester. I think the ground is even.

Edgar. Horrible steep.
Hark, do you hear the sea?

Gloucester. No, truly.

Edgar. Why, then, your other senses grow imperfect
By your eyes' anguish.

Gloucester. So may it be indeed.
I think your voice is altered, and you speak
In better phrase and matter than you did.

Edgar. You're much deceived. In nothing am I changed
But in my garments.

Gloucester. I think you're better spoken.

Edgar. Come on, sir; here's the place. Stand still. How fearful
And dizzy it is to cast one's eyes so low!
The crows and choughs that wing the midway air
Show scarce so gross as beetles. Halfway down
Hangs one that gathers samphire— dreadful trade!
I think he seems no bigger than his head.
The fishermen that walk upon the beach
Appear like mice; and yond tall anchoring bark,
Diminished to her cock; her cock, a buoy
Almost too small for sight. The murmuring surge
That on the unnumbered idle pebble chafes
Cannot be heard so high. I'll look no more,
Lest my brain turn, and the deficient sight
Topple down headlong.

Gloucester. Set me where you stand.

Come on, sir; here's the place. Stand still. How fearful
And dizzy it is to cast one's eyes so low!

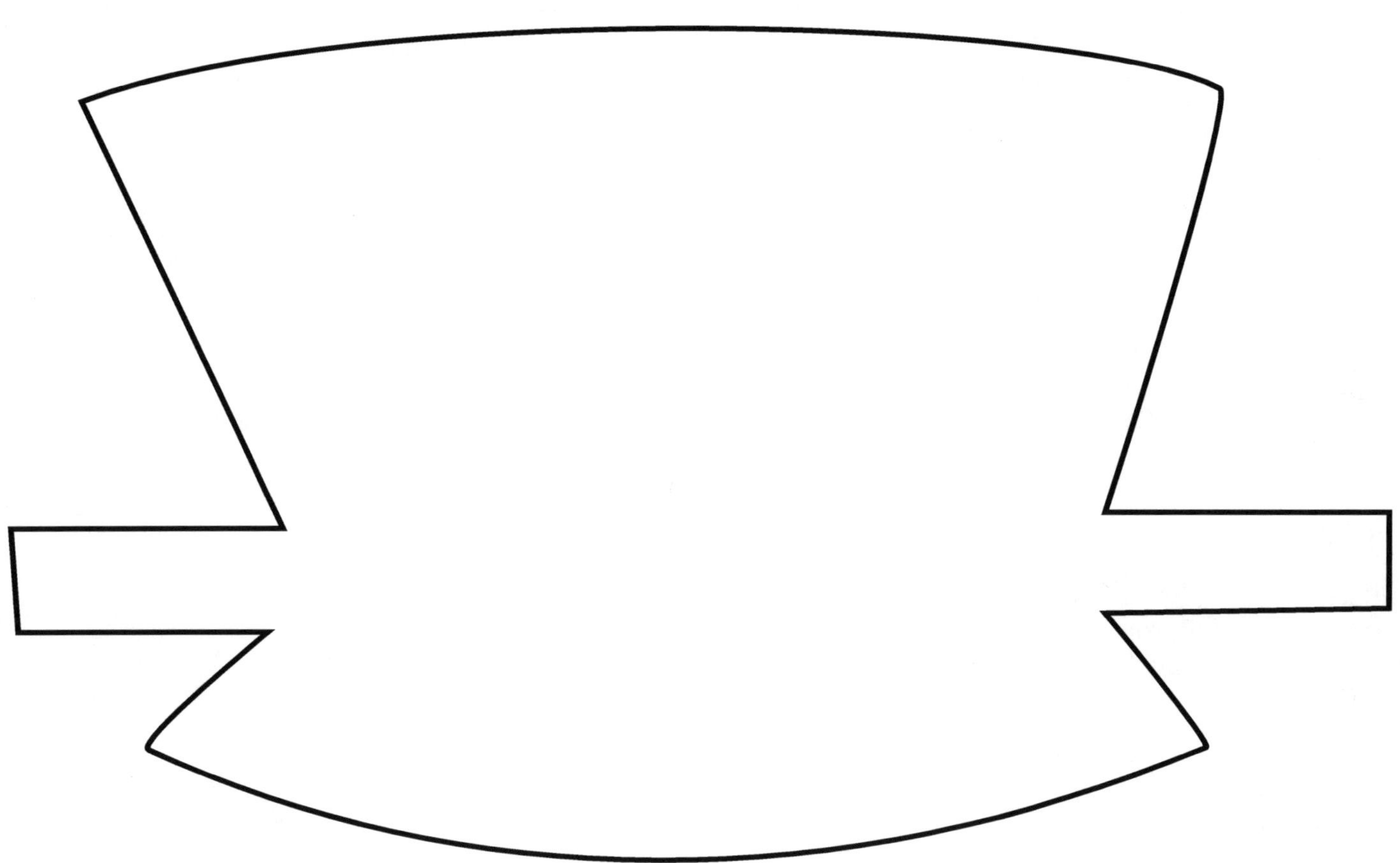

Edgar. Give me your hand. You are now within a foot
Of the extreme verge. For all beneath the moon
Would I not leap upright.

Gloucester. Let go my hand.
Here, friend, is another purse; in it a jewel
Well worth a poor man's taking. Fairies and gods
Prosper it with you! Go you further off;
Bid me farewell, and let me hear you going.

Edgar. Now fare you well, good sir.

Gloucester. With all my heart.

Edgar. [*Aside*]. Why I do trifle thus with his despair
Is done to cure it.

Gloucester. O you mighty gods!

[*He kneels*]

This world I do renounce, and, in your sights,
Shake patiently my great affliction off.
If I could bear it longer and not fall
To quarrel with your great opposeless wills,
My snuff and loathed part of nature should
Burn itself out. If Edgar live, O, bless him!
Now, fellow, fare you well.

[*He falls forward and swoons*]

Edgar. Gone, sir, farewell.—
And yet I know not how conceit may rob
The treasury of life when life itself
Yields to the theft. Had he been where he thought,
By this had thought been past.— Alive or dead?
Ho you, sir! friend! Hear you, sir? Speak!—
Thus might he pass indeed. Yet he revives.
What are you, sir?

Gloucester. Away, and let me die.

Edgar. Had you been aught but gossamer, feathers, air,
So many fathom down precipitating,
You'd shivered like an egg; but you do breathe;
Has heavy substance; bleed not; speak; are sound.
Ten masts at each make not the altitude
Which you have perpendicularly fell.
Your life is a miracle. Speak yet again.

Gloucester. But have I fallen, or no?

This world I do renounce, and, in your sights,
Shake patiently my great affliction off.

Edgar. From the dread summit of this chalky bourn.
Look up a-height. The shrill-gorged lark so far
Cannot be seen or heard. Do but look up.

Gloucester. Alack, I have no eyes!
Is wretchedness deprived that benefit
To end itself by death? It was yet some comfort
When misery could beguile the tyrant's rage
And frustrate his proud will.

Edgar. Give me your arm.
Up— so. How is it? Feel you your legs? You stand.

Gloucester. Too well, too well.

Edgar. This is above all strangeness.
Upon the crown of the cliff what thing was that
Which parted from you?

Gloucester. A poor unfortunate beggar.

Edgar. As I stood here below, I thought his eyes
Were two full moons; he had a thousand noses,
Horns whelked and waved like the enridged sea.
It was some fiend. Therefore, you happy father,
Think that the clearest gods, who make them honors
Of men's impossibility, have preserved you.

Gloucester. I do remember now. Henceforth I'll bear
Affliction till it do cry out itself
"Enough, enough," and die. That thing you speak of,
I took it for a man. Often it would say
"The fiend, the fiend"— he led me to that place.

Edgar. Bear free and patient thoughts.

[*Enter Lear, mad, fantastically dressed with weeds*]

But who comes here?
The safer sense will never accommodate
His master thus.

Lear. No, they cannot touch me for coming;
I am the King himself.

Edgar. O you side-piercing sight!

Lear. Nature is above art in that respect. There's your press money. That fellow handles his bow like a crow-keeper. Draw me a clothier's yard. Look, look, a mouse! Peace, peace; this piece of toasted cheese will do it. There's my gauntlet; I'll prove it on a giant. Bring up the brown bills. O, well flown, bird! in the clout, in the clout! Hewgh! Give the word.

Edgar. Sweet marjoram.

Lear. Pass.

Look up a-height. The shrill-gorged lark so far
Cannot be seen or heard. Do but look up.

Gloucester. I know that voice.

Lear. Ha! Goneril with a white beard? They flattered me like a dog, and told me I had white hairs in my beard before the black ones were there. To say "ay" and "no" to everything I said! "Ay" and "no" too was no good divinity. When the rain came to wet me once, and the wind to make me chatter; when the thunder would not peace at my bidding; there I found 'em, there I smelt 'em out. Go to, they are not men of their words! They told me I was everything. It's a lie— I am not ague-proof.

Gloucester. The trick of that voice I do well remember.
Is it not the King?

Lear. Ay, every inch a king!
When I do stare, see how the subject quakes.
I pardon that man's life. What was your cause?
Adultery?
You shall not die. Die for adultery? No.
The wren goes to it, and the small gilded fly
Does lecher in my sight.
Let copulation thrive; for Gloucester's bastard son
Was kinder to his father than my daughters
Got between the lawful sheets.
To it, luxury, pell-mell! for I lack soldiers.
Behold yond simpering dame,
Whose face between her forks presages snow,
That minces virtue, and does shake the head
To hear of pleasure's name.
The fitchew nor the soiled horse goes to it
With a more riotous appetite.
Down from the waist they are Centaurs,
Though women all above.
But to the girdle do the gods inherit,
Beneath is all the fiend's.
There's hell, there's darkness, there's the sulphurous pit;
burning, scalding, stench, consumption. Fie, fie, fie! pah, pah!
Give me an ounce of civet, good apothecary, to sweeten my imagination. There's money for you.

Gloucester. O, let me kiss that hand!

Lear. Let me wipe it first; it smells of mortality.

Ay, every inch a king!
When I do stare, see how the subject quakes.

Gloucester. O ruined piece of nature! This great world
Shall so wear out to naught. Do you know me?

Lear. I remember your eyes well enough. Do you squiny at me? No, do your worst, blind Cupid! I'll not love. Read you this challenge; mark but the penning of it.

Gloucester. Were all the letters suns, I could not see one.

Edgar. [*Aside*] I would not take this from report. It is,
And my heart breaks at it.

Lear. Read.

Gloucester. What, with the case of eyes?

Lear. O, ho, are you there with me? No eyes in your head, nor no money in your purse? Your eyes are in a heavy case, your purse in a light. Yet you see how this world goes.

Gloucester. I see it feelingly.

Lear. What, are mad? A man may see how the world goes with no eyes. Look with your ears. See how yond justice rails upon yond simple thief. Hark in your ear. Change places and, handy-dandy, which is the justice, which is the thief? You have seen a farmer's dog bark at a beggar?

Gloucester. Ay, sir.

Lear. And the creature run from the cur?
There you might behold the great image of authority: a dog's obeyed in office.
You rascal beadle, hold your bloody hand!
Why do you lash that whore? Strip your own back.
You hotly lusts to use her in that kind
For which you whip her. The usurer hangs the cozener.
Through tattered clothes small vices do appear;
Robes and furred gowns hide all. Plate sin with gold,
And the strong lance of justice hurtless breaks;
Arm it in rags, a pygmy's straw does pierce it.
None does offend, none— I say none! I'll able 'em.
Take that of me, my friend, who have the power
To seal the accuser's lips. Get you glass eyes
And, like a scurvy politician, seem
To see the things you do not. Now, now, now, now!
Pull off my boots. Harder, harder! So.

Edgar. O, matter and impertinency mixed!
Reason, in madness!

What, are mad? A man may see how the world goes with no eyes. Look with your ears.

Lear. If you will weep my fortunes, take my eyes.
I know you well enough; your name is Gloucester.
You must be patient. We came crying here;
You know, the first time that we smell the air
We wawl and cry. I will preach to you. Mark.

Gloucester. Alack, alack the day!

Lear. When we are born, we cry that we are come
To this great stage of fools. This is a good block.
It were a delicate stratagem to shoe
A troop of horse with felt. I'll put it in proof,
And when I have stolen upon these sons-in-law,
Then kill, kill, kill, kill, kill, kill!

[*Enter a Gentleman with Attendants*]

Gentleman. O, here he is! Lay hand upon him.— Sir,
Your most dear daughter—

Lear. No rescue? What, a prisoner? I am even
The natural fool of fortune. Use me well;
You shall have ransom. Let me have a surgeon;
I am cut to the brains.

Gentleman. You shall have anything.

Lear. No seconds? All myself?
Why, this would make a man a man of salt,
To use his eyes for garden waterpots,
Ay, and laying autumn's dust.

Gentleman. Good sir—

Lear. I will die bravely, like a smug bridegroom. What!
I will be jovial. Come, come, I am a king;
My masters, know you that?

Gentleman. You are a royal one, and we obey you.

Lear. Then there's life in it. Nay, an you get it, you shall get it by running. Sa, sa, sa, sa!

[*Exit Lear running. Attendants follow*]

What, a prisoner? I am even
The natural fool of fortune.

Gentleman. A sight most pitiful in the meanest wretch,
Past speaking of in a king! You have one daughter
Who redeems nature from the general curse
Which two have brought her to.

Edgar. Hail, gentle sir.

Gentleman. Sir, speed you. What's your will?

Edgar. Do you hear aught, sir, of a battle toward?

Gentleman. Most sure and vulgar. Every one hears that
Which can distinguish sound.

Edgar. But, by your favor,
How near's the other army?

Gentleman. Near and on speedy foot. The main descry
Stands on the hourly thought.

Edgar. I thank you sir. That's all.

Gentleman. Though that the Queen on special cause is here,
Her army is moved on.

Edgar. I thank you, sir

[*Exit Gentleman*]

Gloucester. You ever-gentle gods, take my breath from me;
Let not my worser spirit tempt me again
To die before you please!

Edgar. Well pray you, father.

Gloucester. Now, good sir, what are you?

Edgar. A most poor man, made tame to fortune's blows,
Who, by the art of known and feeling sorrows,
Am pregnant to good pity. Give me your hand;
I'll lead you to some biding.

Gloucester. Hearty thanks.
The bounty and the benison of heaven
To boot, and boot!

Let not my worser spirit tempt me again
To die before you please!

[*Enter Oswald the Steward*]

Oswald. A proclaimed prize! Most happy!
That eyeless head of yours was first framed flesh
To raise my fortunes. You old unhappy traitor,
Briefly yourself remember. The sword is out
That must destroy you.

Gloucester. Now let your friendly hand
Put strength enough to it.

[*Edgar interposes*]

Oswald. Wherefore, bold peasant,
Dare you support a published traitor? Hence!
Lest that the infection of his fortune take
Like hold on you. Let go his arm.

Edgar. Chill not let go, zir, without vurther 'cagion.

Oswald. Let go, slave, or you diest!

Edgar. Good gentleman, go your gait, and let poor voke pass. An chud ha' bin zwaggered out of my life, 'twould not ha' bin zo long as it is by a vortnight. Nay, come not near the old man. Keep out, che vore you, or Ise try whether your costard or my ballow be the harder. Chill be plain with you.

Oswald. Out, dunghill!

[*They fight*]

Edgar. Chill pick your teeth, zir. Come! No matter vor your foins.

[*Oswald falls*]

Oswald. Slave, you have slain me. Villain, take my purse.
If ever you will thrive, bury my body,
And give the letters which you find about me
To Edmund Earl of Gloucester. Seek him out
Upon the British party. O, untimely death! Death!

[*He dies*]

Dare you support a published traitor? Hence!

Edgar. I know you well. A serviceable villain,
As duteous to the vices of your mistress
As badness would desire.

Gloucester. What, is he dead?

Edgar. Sit you down, father; rest you.
Let's see his pockets; these letters that he speaks of
May be my friends. He's dead. I am only sorry
He had no other deathsman. Let us see.
Leave, gentle wax; and, manners, blame us not.
To know our enemies' minds, we'd rip their hearts;
Their papers, is more lawful.

Reads the letter]

"Let our reciprocal vows be remembered. You have many opportunities to cut him off. If your will want not, time and place will be fruitfully offered. There is nothing done, if he return the conqueror. Then am I the prisoner, and his bed my jail; from the loathed warmth whereof deliver me, and supply the place for your labor. "Your (wife, so I would say) affectionate servant, Goneril"

O indistinguished space of woman's will!
A plot upon her virtuous husband's life,
And the exchange my brother! Here in the sands
You I'll rake up, the post unsanctified
Of murderous lechers; and in the mature time
With this ungracious paper strike the sight
Of the death-practised Duke, For him it is well
That of your death and business I can tell.

Gloucester. The King is mad. How stiff is my vile sense,
That I stand up, and have ingenious feeling
Of my huge sorrows! Better I were distract.
So should my thoughts be severed from my griefs,
And woes by wrong imaginations lose
The knowledge of themselves.

[*A drum afar off*]

Edgar. Give me your hand.
Far off I think I hear the beaten drum.
Come, father, I'll bestow you with a friend.

[*Exeunt*]

[A tent in the French camp]

[Enter Cordelia, Kent, Doctor, and Gentleman]

Cordelia. O you good Kent, how shall I live and work
To match your goodness? My life will be too short
And every measure fail me.

Kent. To be acknowledged, madam, is overpaid.
All my reports go with the modest truth;
Nor more nor clipped, but so.

Cordelia. Be better suited.
These weeds are memories of those worser hours.
please put them off.

Kent. Pardon, dear madam.
Yet to be known shortens my made intent.
My boon I make it that you know me not
Till time and I think meet.

Cordelia. Then be it so, my good lord.
[*To the Doctor*] How, does the King?

Doctor. Madam, sleeps still.

Cordelia. O you kind gods,
Cure this great breach in his abused nature!
The untuned and jarring senses, O, wind up
Of this child-changed father!

Doctor. So please your Majesty
That we may wake the King? He has slept long.

Cordelia. Be governed by your knowledge, and proceed
In the sway of your own will. Is he arrayed?

[Enter Lear in a chair carried by Servants]

Gentleman. Ay, madam. In the heaviness of sleep
We put fresh garments on him.

Doctor. Be by, good madam, when we do awake him.
I doubt not of his temperance.

Cordelia. Very well.

[Music]

To be acknowledged, madam, is overpaid.

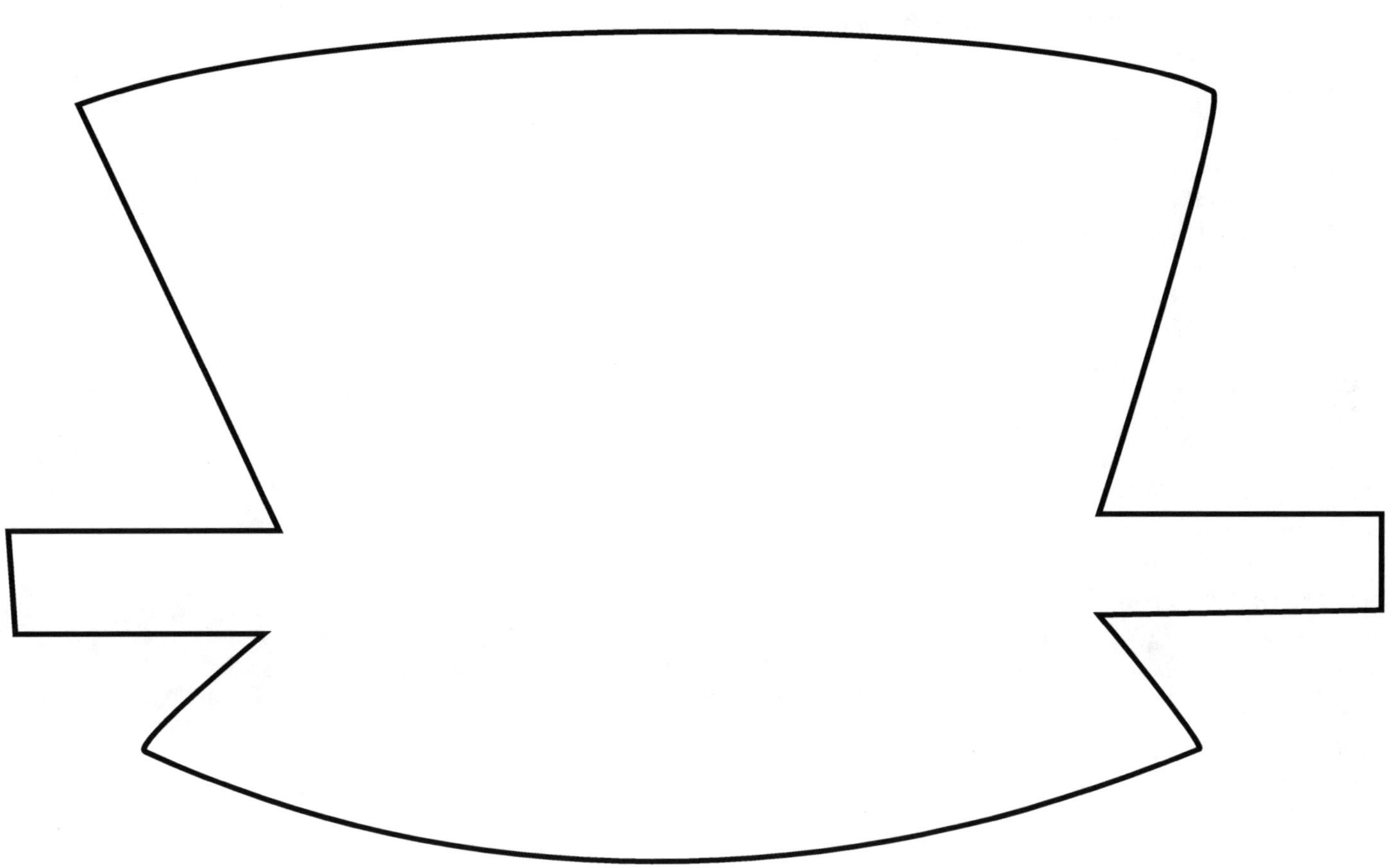

Doctor. Please you draw near. Louder the music there!

Cordelia. O my dear father, restoration hang
Your medicine on my lips, and let this kiss
Repair those violent harms that my two sisters
Have in your reverence made!

Kent. Kind and dear princess!

Cordelia. Had you not been their father, these white flakes
Had challenged pity of them. Was this a face
To be opposed against the warring winds?
To stand against the deep dread-bolted thunder?
In the most terrible and nimble stroke
Of quick cross lightning? to watch— poor perdu!—
With this thin helm? My enemy's dog,
Though he had bit me, should have stood that night
Against my fire; and were you fain, poor father,
To hovel you with swine and rogues forlorn,
In short and musty straw? Alack, alack!
It's wonder that your life and wits at once
Had not concluded all.— He wakes. Speak to him.

Doctor. Madam, do you; it is fittest.

Cordelia. How does my royal lord? How fares your Majesty?

Lear. You do me wrong to take me out of the grave.
You are a soul in bliss; but I am bound
Upon a wheel of fire, that my own tears
Do scald like molten lead.

Cordelia. Sir, do you know me?

Lear. You are a spirit, I know. When did you die?

Cordelia. Still, still, far wide!

Doctor. He's scarce awake. Let him alone awhile.

Lear. Where have I been? Where am I? Fair daylight,
I am mightily abused. I should even die with pity,
To see another thus. I know not what to say.
I will not swear these are my hands. Let's see.
I feel this pin prick. Would I were assured
Of my condition!

Was this a face
To be opposed against the warring winds?

Cordelia. O, look upon me, sir,
And hold your hands in benediction over me.
No, sir, you must not kneel.

Lear. Pray, do not mock me.
I am a very foolish fond old man,
Fourscore and upward, not an hour more nor less;
And, to deal plainly,
I fear I am not in my perfect mind.
I think I should know you, and know this man;
Yet I am doubtful; for I am mainly ignorant
What place this is; and all the skill I have
Remembers not these garments; nor I know not
Where I did lodge last night. Do not laugh at me;
For (as I am a man) I think this lady
To be my child Cordelia.

Cordelia. And so I am! I am!

Lear. Be your tears wet? Yes, faith. I pray weep not.
If you have poison for me, I will drink it.
I know you do not love me; for your sisters
Have, as I do remember, done me wrong.
You have some cause, they have not.

Cordelia. No cause, no cause.

Lear. Am I in France?

Kent. In your own kingdom, sir.

Lear. Do not abuse me.

Doctor. Be comforted, good madam. The great rage
You see is killed in him; and yet it is danger
To make him even over the time he has lost.
Desire him to go in. Trouble him no more
Till further settling.

Cordelia. Will it please your Highness walk?

Lear. You must bear with me.
Pray you now, forget and forgive. I am old and foolish.

[*Exeunt. Remaining Kent and Gentleman*]

I think this lady
To be my child Cordelia.

Gentleman. Holds it true, sir, that the Duke of Cornwall was so slain?

Kent. Most certain, sir.

Gentleman. Who is conductor of his people?

Kent. As it is said, the bastard son of Gloucester.

Gentleman. They say Edgar, his banished son, is with the Earl of Kent in Germany.

Kent. Report is changeable. It's time to look about; the powers of the kingdom approach apace.

Gentleman. The arbitrement is like to be bloody.
Fare you well, sir.

[*Exit Gentleman*]

Kent. My point and period will be thoroughly wrought,
Or well or ill, as this day's battle's fought.

[*Exit Kent*]

Report is changeable. It's time to look about; the powers of the kingdom approach apace.

Act Five

1

[The British camp near Dover]

[Enter, with Drum and Colors, Edmund, Regan, Gentleman, and Soldiers]

Edmund. Know of the Duke if his last purpose hold,
Or whether since he is advised by aught
To change the course. He's full of alteration
And self-reproving. Bring his constant pleasure.

[Exit an Officer]

Regan. Our sister's man is certainly miscarried.

Edmund. Tis to be doubted, madam.

Regan. Now, sweet lord,
You know the goodness I intend upon you.
Tell me— but truly— but then speak the truth—
Do you not love my sister?

Edmund. In honored love.

Regan. But have you never found my brother's way
To the forfended place?

Edmund. That thought abuses you.

Regan. I am doubtful that you have been conjunct
And bosomed with her, as far as we call hers.

Edmund. No, by my honor, madam.

Regan. I never shall endure her. Dear my lord,
Be not familiar with her.

Edmund. Fear me not.
She and the Duke her husband!

Tell me— but truly— but then speak the truth—
Do you not love my sister?

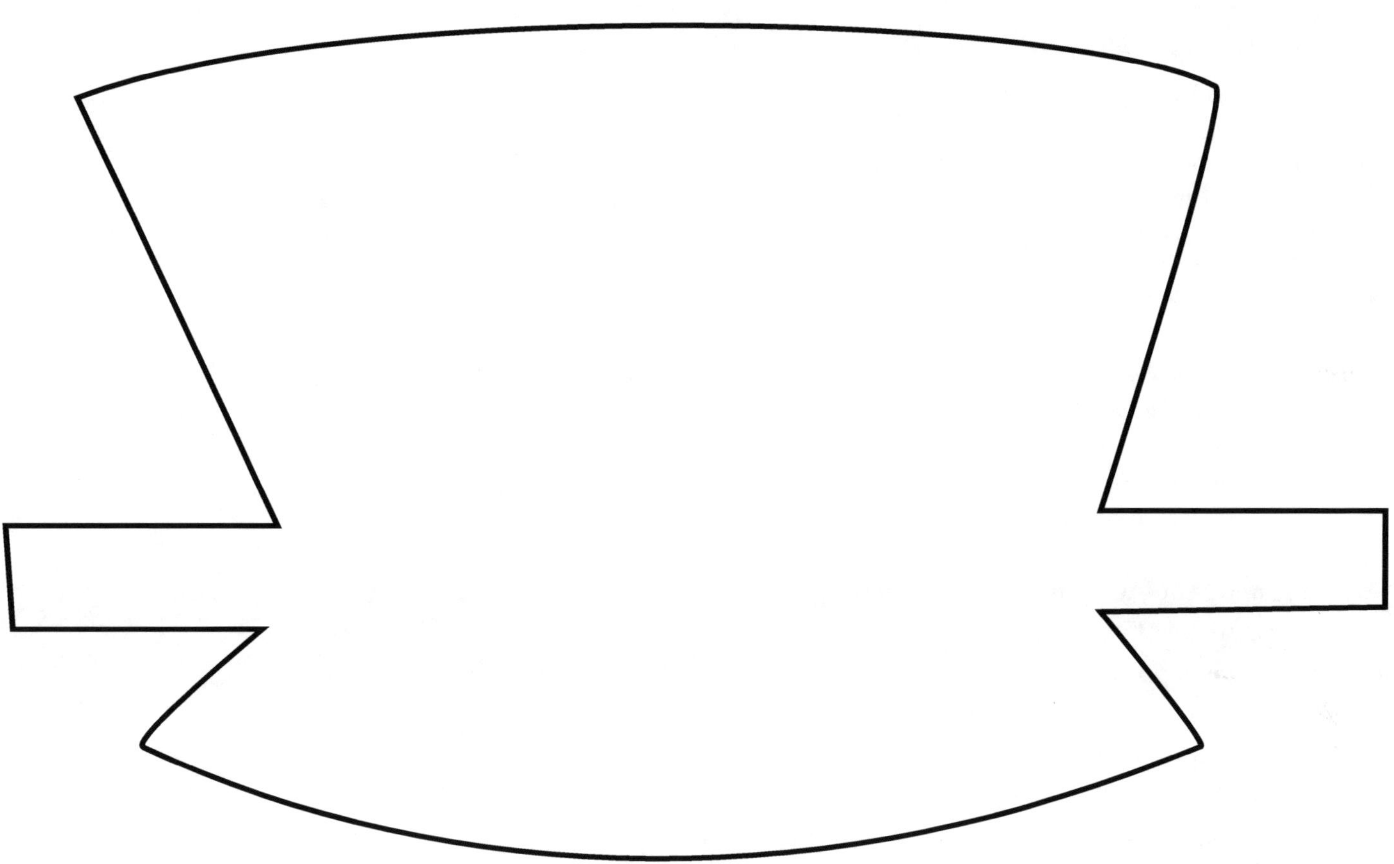

[*Enter, with Drum and Colors, Albany, Goneril, Soldiers*]

Goneril. [*Aside*] I had rather lose the battle than that sister
Should loosen him and me.

Albany. Our very loving sister, well be met.
Sir, this I hear: the King is come to his daughter,
With others whom the rigor of our state
Forced to cry out. Where I could not be honest,
I never yet was valiant. For this business,
It touches us as France invades our land,
Not bolds the King, with others whom, I fear,
Most just and heavy causes make oppose.

Edmund. Sir, you speak nobly.

Regan. Why is this reasoned?

Goneril. Combine together against the enemy;
For these domestic and particular broils
Are not the question here.

Albany. Let's then determine
With the ancient of war on our proceeding.

Edmund. I shall attend you presently at your tent.

Regan. Sister, you'll go with us?

Goneril. No.

Regan. It's most convenient. Pray you go with us.

Goneril. [*Aside*] O, ho, I know the riddle.— I will go.

[*As they are going out, enter Edgar disguised*]

Edgar. If ever your Grace had speech with man so poor,
Hear me one word.

Albany. I'll overtake you.— Speak.

[*Exeunt; all but Albany and Edgar*]

Sir, this I hear: the King is come to his daughter,

Edgar. Before you fight the battle, open this letter.
If you have victory, let the trumpet sound
For him that brought it. Wretched though I seem,
I can produce a champion that will prove
What is avouched there. If you miscarry,
Your business of the world has so an end,
And machination ceases. Fortune love you!

Albany. Stay till I have read the letter.

Edgar. I was forbid it.
When time shall serve, let but the herald cry,
And I'll appear again.

Albany. Why, fare you well. I will overlook your paper.

[*Exit Edgar*]

[*Enter Edmund*]

Edmund. The enemy's in view; draw up your powers.
Here is the guess of their true strength and forces
By diligent discovery; but your haste
Is now urged on you.

Albany. We will greet the time.

[*Exit Albany*]

Edmund. To both these sisters have I sworn my love;
Each jealous of the other, as the stung
Are of the adder. Which of them shall I take?
Both? one? or neither? Neither can be enjoyed,
If both remain alive. To take the widow
Exasperates, makes mad her sister Goneril;
And hardly shall I carry out my side,
Her husband being alive. Now then, we'll use
His countenance for the battle, which being done,
Let her who would be rid of him devise
His speedy taking off. As for the mercy
Which he intends to Lear and to Cordelia—
The battle done, and they within our power,
Shall never see his pardon; for my state
Stands on me to defend, not to debate.

[*Exit Edmund*]

The enemy's in view; draw up your powers

2

[A field between the two camps]

[Alarum within. Enter, with Drum and Colors, the Powers of France over the stage, Cordelia with her Father in her hand, and Exeunt]

[Enter Edgar and Gloucester]

Edgar. Here, father, take the shadow of this tree
For your good host. Pray that the right may thrive.
If ever I return to you again,
I'll bring you comfort.

Gloucester. Grace go with you, sir!

[Exit Edgar]

[Alarum and retreat within]

[Enter Edgar]

Edgar. Away, old man! give me your hand! Away!
King Lear has lost, he and his daughter taken.
Give me your hand! come on!

Gloucester. No further, sir. A man may rot even here.

Edgar. What, in ill thoughts again? Men must endure
Their going hence, even as their coming here;
Ripeness is all. Come on.

Gloucester. And that's true too.

[Exeunt]

Men must endure
Their going hence, even as their coming here;
Ripeness is all. Come on.

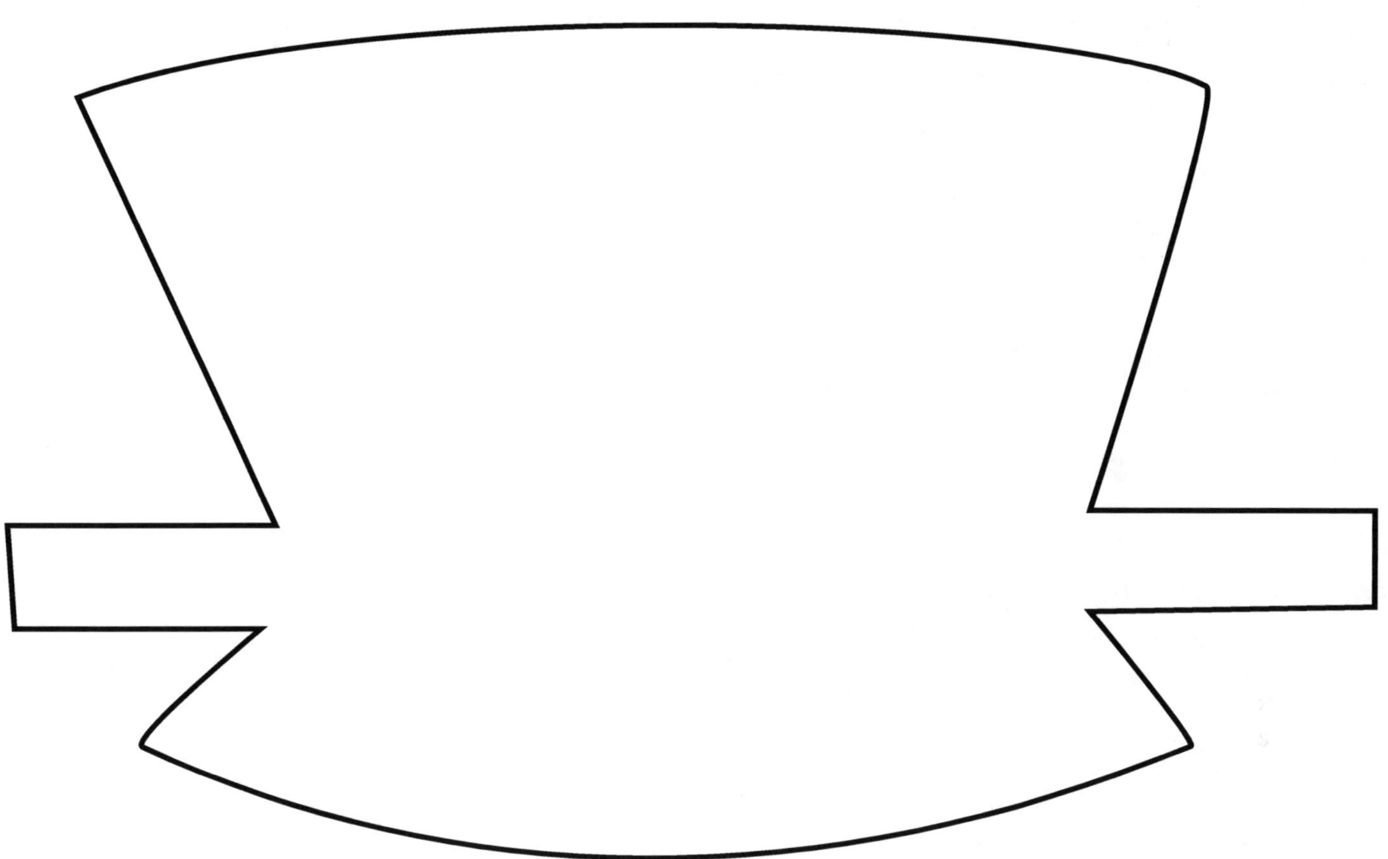

[*The British camp, near Dover*]

[*Enter, in conquest, with Drum and Colors, Edmund; Lear and Cordelia as prisoners; Soldiers, Captain*]

Edmund. Some officers take them away. Good guard
Until their greater pleasures first be known
That are to censure them.

Cordelia. We are not the first
Who with best meaning have incurred the worst.
For you, oppressed king, am I cast down;
Myself could else outfrown false Fortune's frown.
Shall we not see these daughters and these sisters?

Lear. No, no, no, no! Come, let's away to prison.
We two alone will sing like birds in the cage.
When you do ask me blessing, I'll kneel down
And ask of you forgiveness. So we'll live,
And pray, and sing, and tell old tales, and laugh
At gilded butterflies, and hear poor rogues
Talk of court news; and we'll talk with them too—
Who loses and who wins; who's in, who's out—
And take upon us the mystery of things,
As if we were God's spies; and we'll wear out,
In a walled prison, packs and sects of great ones
That ebb and flow by the moon.

Edmund. Take them away.

Lear. Upon such sacrifices, my Cordelia,
The gods themselves throw incense. Have I caught
you?
He that parts us shall bring a brand from heaven
And fire us hence like foxes. Wipe your eyes.
The good years shall devour 'em, flesh and fell,
Before they shall make us weep! We'll see 'em starved
first.
Come.

[*Exeunt Lear and Cordelia, guarded*]

No, no, no, no! Come, let's away to prison.
We two alone will sing like birds in the cage.

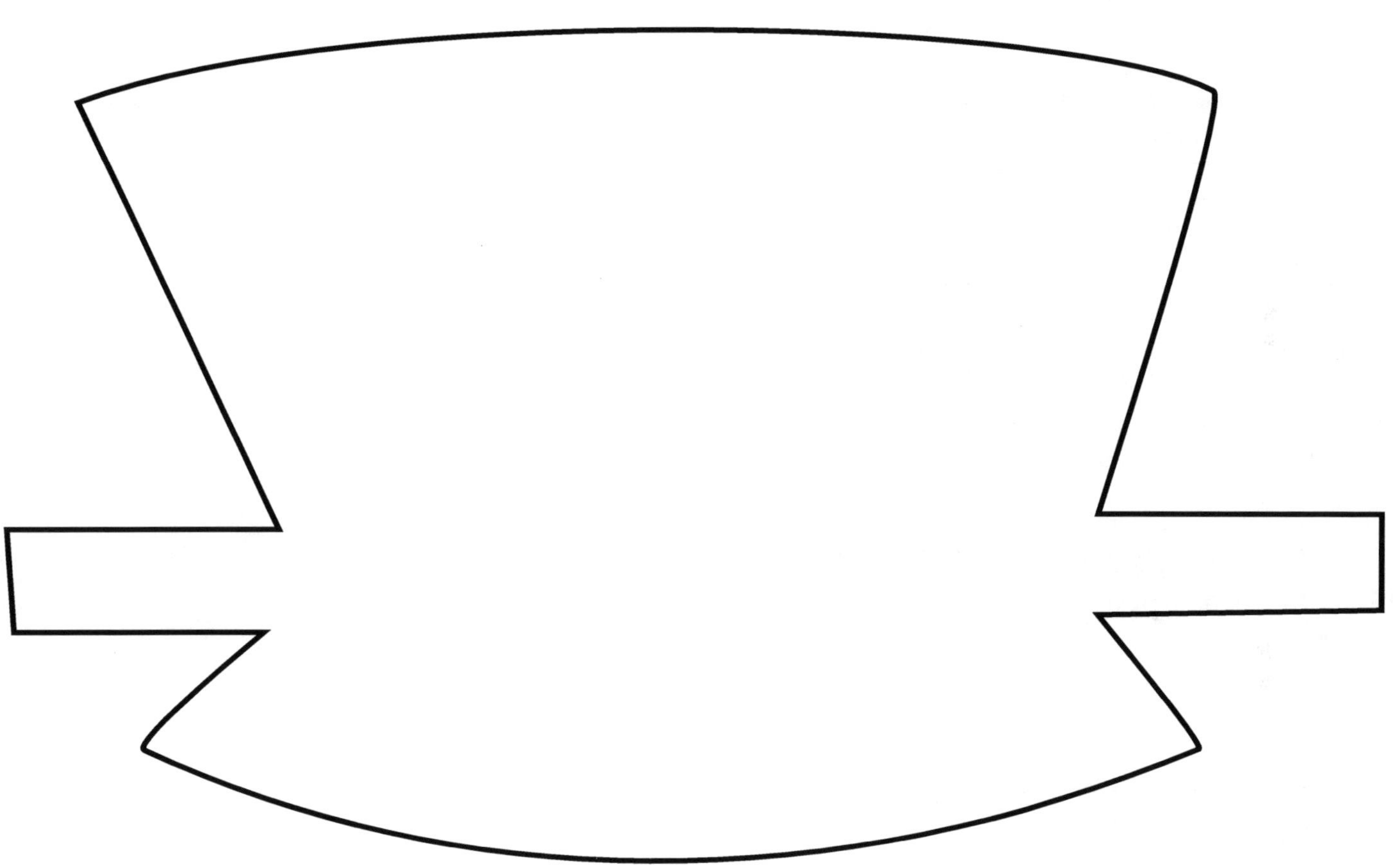

Edmund. Come here, Captain; hark.
Take you this note

[*gives a paper*]

Go follow them to prison.
One step I have advanced you. If you do
As this instructs you, you do make your way
To noble fortunes. Know you this, that men
Are as the time is. To be tender-minded
Does not become a sword. Your great employment
Will not bear question. Either say you'll do it,
Or thrive by other means.

Captain. I'll do it, my lord.

Edmund. About it! and write happy when you have done.
Mark— I say, instantly; and carry it so
As I have set it down.

Captain. I cannot draw a cart, nor eat dried oats;
If it be man's work, I'll do it.

[*Exit*]

[*Flourish. Enter Albany, Goneril, Regan, Soldiers*]

Albany. Sir, you have showed today your valiant strain,
And fortune led you well. You have the captives
Who were the opposites of this day's strife.
We do require them of you, so to use them
As we shall find their merits and our safety
May equally determine.

Edmund. Sir, I thought it fit
To send the old and miserable King
To some retention and appointed guard;
Whose age has charms in it, whose title more,
To pluck the common bosom on his side
And turn our impressed lances in our eyes
Which do command them. With him I sent the Queen,
My reason all the same; and they are ready
Tomorrow, or at further space, to appear
Where you shall hold your session. At this time
We sweat and bleed: the friend has lost his friend;
And the best quarrels, in the heat, are cursed
By those that feel their sharpness.

The question of Cordelia and her father
Requires a fitter place.

Sir, you have showed today your valiant strain,
And fortune led you well.

Albany. Sir, by your patience,
I hold you but a subject of this war,
Not as a brother.

Regan. That's as we list to grace him.
I think our pleasure might have been demanded
Before you had spoke so far. He led our powers,
Bore the commission of my place and person,
The which immediacy may well stand up
And call itself your brother.

Goneril. Not so hot!
In his own grace he does exalt himself
More than in your addition.

Regan. In my rights
By me invested, he compeers the best.

Goneril. That were the most if he should husband you.

Regan. Jesters do oft prove prophets.

Goneril. Holla, holla!
That eye that told you so looked but asquint.

Regan. Lady, I am not well; else I should answer
From a full-flowing stomach. General,
Take you my soldiers, prisoners, patrimony;
Dispose of them, of me; the walls are yours.
Witness the world that I create you here
My lord and master.

Goneril. Mean you to enjoy him?

Albany. The let-alone lies not in your good will.

Edmund. Nor in yours, lord.

Albany. Half-blooded fellow, yes.

Regan. [*to Edmund*] Let the drum strike, and prove my title yours.

Albany. Stay yet; hear reason. Edmund, I arrest you
On capital treason; and, in your attaint,
This gilded serpent

[*points to Goneril*]

For your claim, fair sister,
I bar it in the interest of my wife.
It's she is subcontracted to this lord,
And I, her husband, contradict your banns.
If you will marry, make your loves to me;
My lady is bespoke.

Goneril. An interlude!

Take you my soldiers, prisoners, patrimony;
Dispose of them, of me; the walls are yours.

Albany. You are armed, Gloucester. Let the trumpet sound.
If none appear to prove upon your person
Your heinous, manifest, and many treasons,
There is my pledge!

[*throws down a glove*]

I'll prove it on your heart,
Before I taste bread, you are in nothing less
Than I have here proclaimed you.

Regan. Sick, O, sick!

Goneril. [*Aside*] If not, I'll never trust medicine.

Edmund. There's my exchange

[*throws down a glove*]

What in the world he is
That names me traitor, villain-like he lies.
Call by your trumpet. He that dares approach,
On him, on you, who not? I will maintain
My truth and honor firmly.

Albany. A herald, ho!

Edmund. A herald, ho, a herald!

Albany. Trust to your single virtue; for your soldiers,
All levied in my name, have in my name
Took their discharge.

Regan. My sickness grows upon me.

Albany. She is not well. Convey her to my tent.

[*Exit Regan, led*]

[*Enter a Herald*]

Come here, herald. Let the trumpet sound,
And read out this.

Captain. Sound, trumpet! A trumpet sounds.

Herald. (reads) "If any man of quality or degree within the lists of the army will maintain upon Edmund, supposed Earl of Gloucester, that he is a manifold traitor, let him appear by the third sound of the trumpet. He is bold in his defence."

What in the world he is
That names me traitor, villain-like he lies.

Edmund. Sound! First trumpet.

Herald. Again! Second trumpet.

Herald. Again! Third trumpet.

[*Trumpet answers within*]

[*Enter Edgar, armed, at the third sound, a Trumpet before him*]

Albany. Ask him his purposes, why he appears
Upon this call of the trumpet.

Herald. What are you?
Your name, your quality? and why you answer
This present summons?

Edgar. Know my name is lost;
By treason's tooth bare-gnawn and canker-bit.
Yet am I noble as the adversary
I come to cope.

Albany. Which is that adversary?

Edgar. What's he that speaks for Edmund Earl of Gloucester?

Edmund. Himself. What say you to him?

Edgar. Draw your sword,
That, if my speech offend a noble heart,
Your arm may do you justice. Here is mine.
Behold, it is the privilege of my honors,
My oath, and my profession. I protest—
Maugre your strength, youth, place, and eminence,
Despite your victor sword and fire-new fortune,
Your valor and your heart— you are a traitor;
False to your gods, your brother, and your father;
Conspirant against this high illustrious prince;
And from the extremest upward of your head
To the descent and dust beneath your foot,
A most toad-spotted traitor. Say you "no,"
This sword, this arm, and my best spirits are bent
To prove upon your heart, whereto I speak,
You lie.

Draw your sword,
That, if my speech offend a noble heart,
Your arm may do you justice.

Edmund. In wisdom I should ask your name;
But since your outside looks so fair and warlike,
And that your tongue some say of breeding breathes,
What safe and nicely I might well delay
By rule of knighthood, I disdain and spurn.
Back do I toss those treasons to your head;
With the hell-hated lie overwhelm your heart;
Which— for they yet glance by and scarcely bruise—
This sword of mine shall give them instant way
Where they shall rest forever. Trumpets, speak!

[*Alarums. Fight. Edmund falls*]

Albany. Save him, save him!

Goneril. This is mere practice, Gloucester.
By the law of arms you were not bound to answer
An unknown opposite. You are not vanquished,
But cozened and beguiled.

Albany. Shut your mouth, dame,
Or with this paper shall I stop it.

[*Shows her her letter to Edmund*]

[*To Edmund*] Hold, sir.
[*To Goneril*] You worse than any name, read your own evil.
No tearing, lady! I perceive you know it.

Goneril. Say if I do— the laws are mine, not yours.
Who can arraign me for it?

Albany. Most monstrous!
Know you this paper?

Goneril. Ask me not what I know.

[*Exit*]

Albany. Go after her. She's desperate; govern her.

[*Exit an Officer*]

This sword of mine shall give them instant way
Where they shall rest forever. Trumpets, speak!

Edmund. What, you have charged me with, that have I done,
And more, much more. The time will bring it out.
It's past, and so am I.— But what are you
That have this fortune on me? If you are noble,
I do forgive you.

Edgar. Let's exchange charity.
I am no less in blood than you are, Edmund;
If more, the more you have wronged me.
My name is Edgar and your father's son.
The gods are just, and of our pleasant vices
Make instruments to scourge us.
The dark and vicious place where you he got
Cost him his eyes.

Edmund. You have spoken right; it is true.
The wheel is come full circle; I am here.

Albany. I thought your very gait did prophesy
A royal nobleness. I must embrace you.
Let sorrow split my heart if ever I
Did hate you, or your father!

Edgar. Worthy prince, I know it.

Albany. Where have you hid yourself?
How have you known the miseries of your father?

Edgar. By nursing them, my lord. List a brief tale;
And when it is told, O that my heart would burst!
The bloody proclamation to escape
That followed me so near (O, our lives' sweetness!
That with the pain of death would hourly die
Rather than die at once!) taught me to shift
Into a madman's rags, to assume a semblance
That very dogs disdained; and in this habit
Met I my father with his bleeding rings,
Their precious stones new lost; became his guide,
Led him, begged for him, saved him from despair;
Never (O fault!) revealed myself unto him
Until some half hour past, when I was armed,
Not sure, though hoping of this good success,
I asked his blessing, and from first to last
Told him my pilgrimage. But his flawed heart
(Alack, too weak the conflict to support!)
'Twixt two extremes of passion, joy and grief,
Burst smilingly.

Let's exchange charity.
I am no less in blood than you are, Edmund;

Edmund. This speech of yours has moved me,
And shall perchance do good; but speak you on;
You look as you had something more to say.

Albany. If there be more, more woeful, hold it in;
For I am almost ready to dissolve,
Hearing of this.

Edgar. This would have seemed a period
To such as love not sorrow; but another,
To amplify too much, would make much more,
And top extremity.
While I was big in clamor, came there a man,
Who, having seen me in my worst estate,
Shunned my abhorred society; but then, finding
Who it was that so endured, with his strong arms
He fastened on my neck, and bellowed out
As he'd burst heaven; threw him on my father;
Told the most piteous tale of Lear and him
That ever ear received; which in recounting
His grief grew puissant, and the strings of life
Began to crack. Twice then the trumpets sounded,
And there I left him tranced.

Albany. But who was this?

Edgar. Kent, sir, the banished Kent; who in disguise
Followed his enemy king and did him service
Improper for a slave.

[*Enter a Gentleman with a bloody knife*]

Gentleman. Help, help! O, help!

Edgar. What kind of help?

Albany. Speak, man.

Edgar. What means that bloody knife?

Gentleman. It's hot, it smokes.
It came even from the heart of— O! she's dead!

Albany. Who dead? Speak, man.

Gentleman. Your lady, sir, your lady! and her sister
By her is poisoned; she has confessed it.

Edmund. I was contracted to them both. All three
Now marry in an instant.

Kent, sir, the banished Kent; who in disguise
Followed his enemy king and did him service
Improper for a slave.

[*Enter Kent*]

Edgar. Here comes Kent.

Albany. Produce their bodies, be they alive or dead.

[*Exit Gentleman*]

This judgement of the heavens, that makes us tremble
Touches us not with pity. O, is this he?
The time will not allow the compliment
That very manners urges.

Kent. I am come
To bid my king and master aye good night.
Is he not here?

Albany. Great thing of us forgot!
Speak, Edmund, where's the King? and where's Cordelia?

[*The bodies of Goneril and Regan are brought in*]

See you this object, Kent?

Kent. Alack, why thus?

Edmund. Yet Edmund was beloved.
The one the other poisoned for my sake,
And after slew herself.

Albany. Even so. Cover their faces.

Edmund. I pant for life. Some good I mean to do,
Despite of my own nature. Quickly send
(Be brief in it) to the castle; for my writ
Is on the life of Lear and on Cordelia.
Nay, send in time.

Albany. Run, run, O, run!

Edgar. To who, my lord? Who has the office? Send
Your token of reprieve.

Edmund. Well thought on. Take my sword;
Give it the Captain.

Albany. Haste you for your life.

[*Exit Edgar*]

Yet Edmund was beloved.
The one the other poisoned for my sake,
And after slew herself.

Edmund. He has commission from your wife and me
To hang Cordelia in the prison and
To lay the blame upon her own despair
That she fordid herself.

Albany. The gods defend her! Bear him hence awhile.

[*Edmund is borne off*]

[*Enter Lear, with Cordelia dead in his arms, Edgar, Captain, and others following*]

Lear. Howl, howl, howl, howl! O, you are men of stone.
Had I your tongues and eyes, I'd use them so
That heaven's vault should crack. She's gone forever!
I know when one is dead, and when one lives.
She's dead as earth. Lend me a looking glass.
If that her breath will mist or stain the stone,
Why, then she lives.

Kent. Is this the promised end?

Edgar. Or image of that horror?

Albany. Fall and cease!

Lear. This feather stirs; she lives! If it be so,
It is a chance which does redeem all sorrows
That ever I have felt.

Kent. O my good master!

Lear. Please away!

Edgar. It's noble Kent, your friend.

Lear. A plague upon you, murderers, traitors all!
I might have saved her; now she's gone forever!
Cordelia, Cordelia! stay a little. Ha!
What is it you say, her voice was ever soft,
Gentle, and low— an excellent thing in woman.
I killed the slave that was a-hanging you.

Captain. It's true, my lords, he did.

Lear. Did I not, fellow?
I have seen the day, with my good biting falchion
I would have made them skip. I am old now,
And these same crosses spoil me. Who are you?
Mine eyes are not of the best. I'll tell you straight.

Cordelia, Cordelia! stay a little. Ha!

Kent. If fortune brag of two she loved and hated,
One of them we behold.

Lear. This is a dull sight. Are you not Kent?

Kent. The same—
Your servant Kent. Where is your servant Caius?

Lear. He's a good fellow, I can tell you that.
He'll strike, and quickly too. He's dead and rotten.

Kent. No, my good lord; I am the very man—

Lear. I'll see that straight.

Kent. That from your first of difference and decay
Have followed your sad steps.

Lear. You're welcome here.

Kent. Nor no man else! All's cheerless, dark, and deadly.
Your eldest daughters have fordone themselves,
And desperately are dead.

Lear. Ay, so I think.

Albany. He knows not what he says; and vain is it
That we present us to him.

Edgar. Very bootless.

[*Enter a Captain*]

Captain. Edmund is dead, my lord.

Albany. That's but a trifle here.
You lords and noble friends, know our intent.
What comfort to this great decay may come
Shall be applied. For us, we will resign,
During the life of this old Majesty,
To him our absolute power; [*to Edgar and Kent*] you
to your rights;
With boot, and Such addition as your honors
Have more than merited.— All friends shall taste
The wages of their virtue, and all foes
The cup of their deservings.— O, see, see!

Edmund is dead, my lord.
That's but a trifle here.

Lear. And my poor fool is hanged! No, no, no life!
Why should a dog, a horse, a rat, have life,
And you no breath at all? You'll come no more,
Never, never, never, never, never!
Pray you undo this button. Thank you, sir.
Do you see this? Look on her! look! her lips!
Look there, look there!

[*He dies*]

Edgar. He faints! My lord, my lord!

Kent. Break, heart; please break!

Edgar. Look up, my lord.

Kent. Vex not his ghost. O, let him pass! He hates him
That would upon the rack of this tough world
Stretch him out longer.

Edgar. He is gone indeed.

Kent. The wonder is, he has endured so long.
He but usurped his life.

Albany. Bear them from hence. Our present business
Is general woe.
[*To Kent and Edgar*] Friends of my soul, you two
Rule in this realm, and the gored state sustain.

Kent. I have a journey, sir, shortly to go.
My master calls me; I must not say no.

Albany. The weight of this sad time we must obey,
Speak what we feel, not what we ought to say.
The oldest have borne most; we that are young
Shall never see so much, nor live so long.

[*Exeunt with a dead march*]

Do you see this? Look on her! look! her lips!
Look there, look there!

The End

Contents

afore : before
aidant : helpful
alarum : call to arms
allowance : permitting, allowing
an : if
aroint : get you gone!
atwain : in two
anon : soon
arbitrement : arbitration, settling of a dispute
auricular : overhearing

Bedlam : madhouse; originally, St. Mary of Bethlehem in London, hospital/prison for the demented
beck : beckon
benison : blessing
bewray : disclose; betray
brach : bitch dog

cadent : falling; rhythmic, in waves
caitiff : coward, wretch
carbonado : slice
century : a hundred men
chough : black passerine bird with curved beak
civet : cat with distinctive odor
clotpoll : clodpoll, dolt
compeer : peer, comrade
conjunct : joined, united
contemned : viewed with contempt
continent : with self-restraint
coxcomb : jester's tassled cap; dandy

deboshed : debauched
disnatured : unnatural

disquantity : reduce in numbers

Epicurism : pursuit of pleasure
esperance : hope

fain : prefer, incline to
faithed : honest, sincere
falchion : short broadsword
fastened : clinging, concentrated
festinate : hasty
fitchew : polecat
forefended : forbidden; defended
frontlet : forehead
fumiter : fumitory, herb with small purple flowers

gad : hurriedly; willy-nilly
gast : frighten, scare
germens : germs, seeds

ingraffed : inserted, engraved
intrinse : tight, intricate

jakes : privy, latrine
joint-stool : folding stool

kibes : inflamed heel; ulcerated chilblain
knap : chip; bite

lanch : launch, thrust
lym : dog leash

maugre : despite; in spite of
meiny : household

nighted : darkened, clouded
nuncle : uncle; old man

oeillades : seductive glances
oft : often

packings : preparations
peascod : peapod
pelting : paltry
perdu : soldier on hazardous mission
perdy : truly
perforce : by necessity
pight : determined, fixed
placket : woman's skirt pocket
plain : complain
pudder : bustle; tumult

questrist : pursuer

ratsbane : rat poison
raze : take away; destroy
remotion : removal
reposal : at rest, tranquillity

sallet : helmet with guard for back of the neck; perhaps mistaken or colloquial for "salad"
samphire : seacliff-clinging fibrous plant
scape : escape
sectary : believer
sequent : following
shealed : shelled; sheltered
simular : sham, pretender
Smulkin : a demon
snuffs : sniffing out
squiny : squint
succeed : proceed, go forward

sumpter : mule, pack animal

superflux : overabundance

Tom o' Bedlam : (from the poem) street person feigning madness, to beg money or get out of difficulties

treacher : traitor, cheat

trow : think, believe; suppose

Turlygod : mad beggar

weal : welfare

wont : accustomed; desired

Author

WILLIAM SHAKESPEARE, *the third of eight children, was born on April 23, 1564 in the English market town of Stratford-upon-Avon. His father became the mayor of Stratford in 1568 and worked as a glovemaker and a moneylender. Four years after leaving school at approximately the age of fourteen, Shakespeare married Anne Hathaway in November of 1582; their first child Susannah was born in May of the following year. Two years later, Anne gave birth to twins, Hamnet and Judith. Between 1585 and 1592, a period called "the lost years," there is almost no evidence about Shakespeare's life, nor is there any solid evidence about how or why he made his way to London to become a dramatist. By 1592, however, Shakespeare's reputation as a playwright and poet had begun to grow. In 1594, he helped found a new theater company, the Lord Chamberlain's Men, and became the company's dramatist. Shakespeare's success increased, and by 1598, the year he registered* The Merchant of Venice, *he had already purchased one of the biggest residences in Stratford. Some of Shakespeare's richest dramatic work was written after the founding of the Globe Theater by the Lord Chamberlain's Men in 1599, including* Julius Caesar, Hamlet, Othello, King Lear, *and* Macbeth. *After 1611, Shakespeare largely retired from the theater to spend more time in Stratford. He died in 1616 on his birthday, April 23, when he was fifty-two years old.*

Editor

SASHA "BIRDIE" NEWBORN *was born in 1940 in Mason City , Iowa. A lover of books from an early age, he read voraciously. Though attending MIT for two years, he finally turned to literature in earnest, earning an MA degree from the University of Iowa. After two years in the Peace Corps in Tanzania as a schoolteacher, he returned to Iowa City and became editor of an "underground newspaper,"* Middle Earth, *then joined Liberation News Service in Massachusetts (1967), before settling in New York City, and learning publishing from the bottom up. In Santa Barbara, California, he became a partner in a poetry press, Mudborn Press, and as an outgrowth of that, launched Bandanna Books in 1981, to serve the college market. In the mid 1990s, "he" became "she," and continues BBooks as well as Mudborn titles to this day.*

Producer

The Producer is the Business Manager; this person is responsible for money matters. That starts with the budget. The Producer must be satisfied that the Budget is realistic, in order for the show to go on.

Some items will be estimates on future earnings, such as ticket sales. If income falls short of expenses, who is the surety that the bills will be paid? If not the Producer, then it must be someone whom the Producer has enlisted.

If the production is intended to be a profit-making venture, then the Budget is more open-ended, to include continuing expenses vs. continuing revenues, until a point is reached at which it becomes no longer economical to continue.

Next is the program or playbill, the booklet handed out at the performance, which ought to look good enough as a souvenir of a wonderful evening. The program is also an important sales tool; it presumably will be filled with advertising paid by sponsors, as well as all the relevant data of the performance—cast, with bios and pictures of the major players, the crew, the staff, supporters, anyone who should be given credit for helping the production.

Publicity also falls in the domain of the Producer, which is essentially the same task as creating the program, but honed for direct mail or email to prospective audience members.

Budget

Income

- Sponsors
- Anticipated ticket sales
- Program ads
- Donors
- Institutional support
- Subscriptions
- Other

Expenses

- Sets and Props
- Costumes
- Theater rental
- Talent
- Contract labor
- Equipment rental
- Program design, printing, mailing
- Advertising
- Ushers and Box Office
- Other

Balance

Playbill

This can be your primary fundraising tool, so make it look as professional as possible.

Synopsis of the play

Possibly a glossary for Italian, Latin, and/or quaint British expressions

Playwright, history of the play (if available)

Director, previous accomplishments

Staff, likewise

Bios of the leading players, with photos

Credits for the cast,
and everyone associated with the production

Space to highlight major donors and sponsors

Design and typesetting (can you get this whole job donated in exchange for ad space?)

Selling ad space

Cover design

Design ads (if necessary)

Printing (perhaps donated in exchange for ad recognition?)

Publicity

Press release

mailing list (if available)

email list

parents (if applicable)

school or institution

paid ads

word-of-mouth

announcements (i.e. auditions)

Box Office, Ushers, Ticket-takers

Pre-Production

Pre-Production has to do with all those physical pieces that have to be acquired or built before performance: sets, costumes, props, equipment, and the theater itself.

The Set Designer and Costume Designer operate more or less independently to produce their pieces, on consultation with the Director as to the effect desired in each scene. Often, the Set Designer also handles or creates the props.

Costumes can be a very creative area, depending on in which time period or fantasy setting that the Director chooses to situate the play. Characters who appear in disguise as well as themselves are a special challenge.

Checking on the equipment and the theater ordinarily is the responsibility of the Stage Manager.

Props

set furniture

swords

trees

beards, mustaches

articles of war

trumpet

wind machine (?)

curtains

Set Design

Shakespeare set the time as in the distant past to his own, which allows for creative construction of a "world." Directors for modern audiences have much more leeway in the visual and palpable presentation of time and space.

The director's vision of the play ideally connects Shakespeare's themes with modern sensibilities. Your coherent vision must drive the whole production, from costumes and sets to the dramatic actions, perhaps the regional accents, references to recent local events in the news. Shakespeare's recurring theme of love explores the extreme of jealousy, exploited by Iago, as a vulnerability. The unlikely coupling of a woman who had scorned marriage up to that point, with a man who scarcely knew how to woo, sets the stage for strong wills to collide—even before Iago's machinations are set in motion.

King Lear offers special challenges for the Set Designer, going from palace scenes to the blasted and windy heath, to war camps. Gloucester at the "cliff" might be creative. With shifting loyalties and disguised intentions, shadows or colored lighting may be useful. Is a scene to be played for comedy or for grief (or both at once)?—confer with the director.

Every scene starts with a stage diagram, for placement of sets and actors' marks. Confer with director for scene requirements.

Act One

1 *King Lear's Palace*

2 *The Earl of Gloucester's Castle*

3 *The Duke of Albany's Palace*

4 *The Duke of Albany's Palace*

5 *Court before the Duke of Albany's Palace*

Act Two

1 *A court within the Castle of the Earl of Gloucester*

2 *Before Gloucester's Castle*

3 *The open country*

4 *Before Gloucester's Castle*

Act Three

1 *A heath. Storm continues*

2 *Another part of the heath*

3 *Gloucester's Castle*

4 *The heath. Before a hovel*

5 *Gloucester's Castle*

6 *A farmhouse near Gloucester's Castle*

7 *Gloucester's Castle*

Act Four

1 *The heath*

2 *Before the Duke of Albany's Palace*

3 *The French camp near Dover*

4 *The French camp*

5 *Gloucester's Castle*

6 *The country near Dover*

7 *A tent in the French camp*

Act Five

1 *The British camp near Dover*

2 *A field between the two camps*

3 *The British camp, near Dover*

Costumes

Not only are there many costumes to make or acquire, some actors will be playing double roles, which need separate costumes. Major players may have an understudy. Costumes are a big deal with Shakespeare productions; they can be creative, educational, or just fun. Two major characters (Edgar and Kent) appear as themselves and also in disguise—but still identifiable to the audience. Design for your budget.

If costumes are to be created from scratch, then actors must be measured as appropriate. Additional measurements for some roles may be required for hat size, shoe size, gloves.

Lear
Height: Inseam: Waist:
Hips: Bust/chest: Arm:
Shoulders:

Lear understudy
Height: Inseam: Waist:
Hips: Bust/chest: Arm:
Shoulders:

Edmund
Height: Inseam: Waist:
Hips: Bust/chest: Arm:
Shoulders:

Edgar
Height: Inseam: Waist:
Hips: Bust/chest: Arm:
Shoulders:

Gloucester
Height: Inseam: Waist:
Hips: Bust/chest: Arm:
Shoulders:

Goneril
Height: Inseam: Waist:
Hips: Bust/chest: Arm:
Shoulders:

Regan
Height: Inseam: Waist:
Hips: Bust/chest: Arm:
Shoulders:

Cordelia
Height: Inseam: Waist:
Hips: Bust/chest: Arm:
Shoulders:

Cornwall
Height: Inseam: Waist:
Hips: Bust/chest: Arm:
Shoulders:

Albany
Height: Inseam: Waist:
Hips: Bust/chest: Arm:
Shoulders:

Burgundy
Height: Inseam: Waist:
Hips: Bust/chest: Arm:
Shoulders:

France
Height: Inseam: Waist:
Hips: Bust/chest: Arm:
Shoulders:

Kent
Height: Inseam: Waist:
Hips: Bust/chest: Arm:
Shoulders:

Fool
Height: Inseam: Waist:
Hips: Bust/chest: Arm:
Shoulders:

Oswald
Height: Inseam: Waist:
Hips: Bust/chest: Arm:
Shoulders:

Knight
Height: Inseam: Waist:
Hips: Bust/chest: Arm:
Shoulders:

Gentleman
Height: Inseam: Waist:
Hips: Bust/chest: Arm:
Shoulders:

Curan
Height: Inseam: Waist:
Hips: Bust/chest: Arm:
Shoulders:

Old Man
Height: Inseam: Waist:
Hips: Bust/chest: Arm:
Shoulders:

Doctor
Height: Inseam: Waist:
Hips: Bust/chest: Arm:
Shoulders:

Herald
Height: Inseam: Waist:
Hips: Bust/chest: Arm:
Shoulders:

Captains
Height: Inseam: Waist:
Hips: Bust/chest: Arm:
Shoulders:

Extras and Groups

Officers
Height: Inseam: Waist:
Hips: Bust/chest: Arm:
Shoulders:

Soldiers
Height: Inseam: Waist:
Hips: Bust/chest: Arm:
Shoulders:

Messenger
Height: Inseam: Waist:
Hips: Bust/chest: Arm:
Shoulders:

Attendants
Height: Inseam: Waist:
Hips: Bust/chest: Arm:
Shoulders:

Stage Management

The Stage Manager's domain is primarily the "Wizard of Oz" position: unseen backstage, but in control of the whole stage, as well as lighting and sound. The task is to coordinate all the elements other than the actors, which includes moving sets on and off the stage, prompting actors if they forget their lines, calling for curtain rise and fall, making sure actors are ready when needed.

A Stage Manager needs to be in communication with the lighting and sound person(s), the stage hands, prompters, actors, musicians (or audio).

The prompter stands behind a side curtain, ready to prompt an actor who misses a line. One prompter on each side is even better.

Stage hands move the scenery around between scenes, and usually are not visible to the audience. Cleverly constructed sets are sturdily built on wheels, in such dimensions as will fit backstage. Got a revolving platform? Great, that's handy for changing whole sets.

Whatever comes up unexpectedly during the play—a set flat falls over, a light burns out—that's the Stage Manager's new task.

Manager

Prompters

Stage Hands

Lighting

Sound

Photography/video

Other

Scheduling

The Schedule is determined by the Director, but is usually handled by an aide, or the Assistant Director (if there is one).

Everyone is on the schedule—where they should be and when. A few points on the schedule are fixed, such as the performance dates. Everything else is geared toward the first night of performance.

A useful technique is to work backward from First Night, to figure how long it will take to get X ready, which may be decided in a conference of the responsible parties. The producer may require certain firm commitments before moving forward. The set designer, the wardrobe department, the stage manager may need to find enough personnel to handle their duties in a reasonable time frame.

The Director must determine, given the available resources and people, how long is an adequate period of time to make it all jell—not just the actors but the whole company. Ideally, this decision is a joint one, agreeable to all parties, to maximize coordination of efforts.

Here is a possible sequence of activities:

Production Timeline

Determination that the play is economically feasible

Decision to do the play

Gather team

Team leaders estimate time required

Build timeline schedule

Pick tentative dates for performance

Verify theater availability

Recruit volunteers and begin work

2nd or 3rd week — is the schedule still looking good?

Plunge ahead

Firm up performance dates, hire theater

Midpoint evaluation (point of no return)

set the clock on tasks behind schedule

arrange alternate plan

Doublecheck each area

publicity campaign in action

- press release
- radio spots
- interviews
- emails

Troubleshooting snags

Invite reviewers

Final runthrough rehearsal

Performance - first night

Following nights—correct rough spots

Wrap party and congratulations

Made in the USA
Las Vegas, NV
17 May 2024